A Common Sense Guide to

Financial Independence

FINANCIAL WISDOM
FOR MY CHILDREN

Choon Then

Dedication

To my children,

All your financial needs, I hope you find them here.

Be careful with your money.
Since I can't nag you forever, that's why I wrote this book.

Foreword

This book contains the basics about investing that I want to teach my children who are now young adults. You can do the same for your children and may wish to share it with those who:

- are in their teens

- have just entered the workforce

- have just started a young family, and are worrying if they and their loved ones, will know how to sustain themselves

- aspire to be financially independent.

This is not meant to be an exhaustive 'all-you-need-to-know' book. It does, however, attempt to take a holistic approach to personal financial management. It highlights the key aspects of money management and provides the foundations for continuous, lifelong learning. I would also propose that clear financial goals are set and monitored to ensure success.

It is important to note that money management is generally a proactive, rather than a passive activity. No amount of dreaming or talking is going to get you to your goals. Concrete action is required. This book contains narratives that provide the basic concepts and should demonstrate their relevance in investing. More in-depth information is easily accessible online. The tables have been deliberately simplified for illustrative purposes; to demonstrate the concepts in financial terms, so that they become vivid. You are encouraged to change the parameters in the spreadsheets, where possible, to better match your situation, matching them to your most realistic financial situation. As you measure your progress through this journey, you will hopefully become more and more motivated to stick to the plan, and possibly even exceed your expectations.

We only have one chance in life to live happily and meaningfully. Financial independence brings a freedom that you could never imagine. But financial independence requires financial literacy. An important part of this process requires starting early to enhance your chances of success. Common sense, discipline, and knowledge all require time to take root. Investment needs time to bear the expected fruit. Luck, to some extent, also plays a part but it is not something that you can control. I have tried to focus on the issues which are under your control.

Contents

Write to email **choonthen123@gmail** for an auto-reply link to downloadable spreadsheets.

Chapter 1

The Foundations – Live a Simple Life, Stay Healthy and Invest in Yourself

Before we even start to invest, your outlook in life needs to be correct. Otherwise, you will never be content. Personal financial management is a lifelong process and a skill, requiring lifelong discipline.

In an increasingly complex and confusing world there is one philosophy that has always stood me in good stead. **Learn to live a simple life.** I believe that by adopting this philosophy you will establish the foundations of happiness and the beginnings of an effective personal financial strategy. As a person of Chinese heritage, I have to say that the over-emphasis on wealth within Chinese culture needs to change. For many people the ultimate goal of a good education is simply to ensure a well-paying job rather than a fulfilling career. Even the Chinese form of greeting means wishing someone wealth and prosperity! The days of starvation and deprivation are no longer acute, at least for many in the developed world. It is time to encourage real success and make real happiness the end goal.

The pursuit of wealth is seldom satiable. It is like a scorecard – the higher it climbs, the more boastful one becomes. The culture of obsession with wealth is not a good one and can even be harmful. It can consume one so completely that the pursuit of a more meaningful and satisfying life is superseded by the pursuit of wealth. A wealthy life is not synonymous with a happy life. Our children's happiness should be more important than simply attaining wealth.

Parents have the most influential role. As parents, we want our children to have ideals, to be noble, to be of good character. Parents should be just as proud of good children as they are of wealthy children. In fact, persons of good moral character are more acceptable in most places and tend to be more successful, even in a less developed society. We want to teach our children to enjoy the simple things in life – a walk on the beach, hiking, cycling, gathering with friends and loved ones. We want to enjoy the beauty in life – in love, the arts, travel. What could be more beautiful and meaningful than love? Romantic love/family love/friendship/filial piety are all essential. Or we could also find beauty in the arts – reading, music, museums, performances, exhibitions. Hardly any of these costs much to enjoy.

What's the difference between owning $10m and $10b anyway? You can't be more comfortable if you are already very comfortable, unless you are seeking vanity. We want our children and our loved ones to have a peaceful and happy life; ok, maybe even a comfortable life, but do we really wish them to have an extravagant life?

So we need to temper our expectations. We have to cultivate good habits and good discipline. Being content then becomes easier, as greed will be kept in check, investment becomes more rational, and success in investing becomes a lot less risky and more assured.

Stay healthy

If you have to choose between health and wealth, for yourself or your children, which will it be? There is no point in having a lot of money without good health to enjoy it. In fact, poor health would be a financial drain on the family. With good health, there will always be more zest for life and the energy to maximize one's potential. We can strive for both, but not at the expense of one for the other. While the outcome is sometimes unpredictable, much can be done to stay healthy.

Practice common sense, which often encompasses going back to basics. Try and cultivate the following:

- be balanced and moderate

- follow medical and health advice

- do no harm to your body, i.e. avoid overindulging

- avoid harmful habits and substances

- avoid an unhealthy lifestyle

- eat healthily and naturally

- have discipline

- develop good habits

- don't take chances and unnecessary risks

- engage in wholesome activities.

Invest in yourself

Many people are unfortunate enough to live in countries that wallow in perpetual poverty. These countries have no immediate prospects, many of their citizens are stuck in the poverty trap. They see no prospect of breaking out for their children, for generation after generation.

The only way out in these circumstances is not handouts, but education. A good education is one of the best investments one can make for ourselves and our children.

Education comes first and foremost with the desire to learn. This involves investing one's time and money. If a hefty school fee is unaffordable, try taking short courses. This might be with a local school or college, or through online courses. The growth of online learning now provides a huge range of opportunities for self-improvement. You can take a look at sites such as Udemy, edX, Coursera or LinkedIn Learning. Many of these sites even offer short courses for free. The key point is that you should learn. If one can read and listen, one can learn. The desire to learn must come from the students, money can help to facilitate it.

Parents can create the environment for learning, no matter what the economic situation. Once children start to read and learn, the world is their oyster. They have the chance to do better than their country, perhaps even go somewhere else better. It may take a bit longer but the prospect is real.

Education promises not just better-paying jobs with economic benefits, more importantly, it boosts the propensity to learn and helps with the ability to think and understand values, i.e. to be a better person. With so much knowledge and sharing online, the world is at our fingertips. If we cannot afford the expense, then invest the time. There are no more excuses for being ignorant unless we choose to be.

Every year the pace of change in the world seems to accelerate. In order to keep up, it is imperative that we continue to grow through continuous, lifelong learning. This should be led by curiosity and inquisitiveness and driven by a desire to better oneself. Try and develop multiple skills; continue to upskill and constantly aim to re-invent oneself.

Key to this development is reading. Make sure you read widely, for, in those writings, there is wisdom embedded and models worth emulating. Observe and listen attentively and humbly, for there are many smart people out there who are keen to share their experiences and wisdom.

Armed with an education and the right mindset, we are now ready to apply ourselves to invest in the right way.

Chapter 2
Start Financial Literacy Early

We worry for our children. We feed them, educate them, protect them. We teach them basic hygiene, send them to school, teach them how to cook, and in some cases, even help pick their future husbands/wives for them! Sooner or later though, they have to stand on their own two feet and look after themselves and their own families, through good times and bad. We worry if they will cope when we are gone. This is why financial literacy is one of the most important life skills. I am at a loss as to why this is not given due focus by parents and schools.

A parent's plan to hand down all the hard-earned wealth accumulated throughout a life of work is because of the love you have for your children. But you don't know if they can handle it. Money is not made in one day but it can surely be squandered in less. They are young, and they do not yet fully understand the jungle in which they are living.

Teaching our children financial literacy has to start early; well before they enter the job market. There are two important aspects to it: 1) knowledge and 2) habits.

Knowledge is the easy part but habits take time to take root. So, parents have to make sure to inculcate these in them from an early age. These habits include:

- being careful with money
- avoiding expensive tastes
- budgeting
- spending on what is needed, not wanted
- enjoying the simple things in life
- the virtue of hard and honest work

- the joy of giving rather than receiving

- avoiding a materialistic outlook.

You can never be too young or too old to start financial literacy. If you are still young, seize the opportunity to greatly improve your chances of earlier financial independence. If you are more mature, there is still a lot that can be done. You can be smarter about your finances going forward and improve your current financial situation. If you are planning to leave money for your children, your investment time horizon is not limited to your lifetime but extended to theirs after you have moved on.

If you are a teacher or a lecturer, you try your best to teach your students all the knowledge possible to build their dream careers. There are people who work themselves to death in some countries, often because they have basic needs to meet. There are people who are so career-minded they neglect the more important things in life, ruining their health and family life. If they have learned not just to do their job and be paid for it, but also to take care of their money and make it grow, they will be able to enjoy the fruits of their wisdom later in life.

If you are a team leader, a departmental head, or a corporate leader, it is not enough to just treat your associates as people whom you pay in return for their efforts. We can act as mentors in so many ways, not just in passing on the skills that colleagues could acquire to do their jobs better. We want them to feel that their work-life balance is actually contributing to their personal life. It is therefore important that we mentor them in personal financial management. Otherwise, they are more likely to constantly complain about not being paid enough, no matter how much bonus you have paid, or how much merit increments have been dished out.

Chapter 3
Start Investing Early

If you want a big tree, you need to give it time to grow. It is the same with investing. If you save $10k per year, then in 10 years you should have $100k and in 30 years that would be $300k, even if you make no gains at all from it. The longer we save, the more time we allow the saving to accumulate. So, it is easy to see why investing early is important, so that we have the most to count on when we retire.

However, that is not the full story. The compounding effect results in a much bigger pie at the end of a long period. (The compounding effect is the ability of an asset to generate earnings, which are then reinvested to also generate its own earnings) – see Chapter 10: The effect of compounding.

Things also get a little more exciting when you add in another factor – international market investing. There are many countries that are well run; consequently, their economies and their stock markets consistently perform well over the long run. In today's connected world, investing in these economies has never been easier. So, you are no longer limited to investing in just your own country, which perhaps may have been underperforming for years. Instead, almost anyone can access any market anywhere in the world to take advantage of better returns, and see their wealth grow over time. Naturally, the longer you invest, the bigger the investment pie.

Let's illustrate this with an example – see Illustration 1 below. If you start investing early, let's say at age 30, in an ETF (an Exchange-Traded Fund, is a basket of securities that tracks an index, sector, commodity, or other assets; that can be traded on a stock exchange just like the publicly traded stocks), with an average annual return of 10%, your asset value will be $174k in 30 years' time, when you retire at 60. If you start late, say at age 50, with only 10 years before retiring at 60, to reach the same goal of the asset value of $174k, your investment return will have to be at an annual compound rate of return of 33.1%. That is unlikely to happen.

Illustration 1

Investing Early: 30 years				
Year	Age	Starting Balance ($)	Return (%)	Asset Value After Return ($)
1	30	10,000	10.0%	11,000
2	31	11,000	10.0%	12,100
3	32	12,100	10.0%	13,310
4	33	13,310	10.0%	14,641
5	34	14,641	10.0%	16,105
6	35	16,105	10.0%	17,716
7	36	17,716	10.0%	19,487
8	37	19,487	10.0%	21,436
9	38	21,436	10.0%	23,579
10	39	23,579	10.0%	25,937
11	40	25,937	10.0%	28,531
12	41	28,531	10.0%	31,384
13	42	31,384	10.0%	34,523
14	43	34,523	10.0%	37,975
15	44	37,975	10.0%	41,772
16	45	41,772	10.0%	45,950
17	46	45,950	10.0%	50,545
18	47	50,545	10.0%	55,599
19	48	55,599	10.0%	61,159
20	49	61,159	10.0%	67,275
21	50	67,275	10.0%	74,002
22	51	74,002	10.0%	81,403
23	52	81,403	10.0%	89,543
24	53	89,543	10.0%	98,497
25	54	98,497	10.0%	108,347
26	55	108,347	10.0%	119,182
27	56	119,182	10.0%	131,100
28	57	131,100	10.0%	144,210
29	58	144,210	10.0%	158,631
30	59	158,631	10.0%	174,494

Investing Early: 10 years				
Year	Age	Starting Balance ($)	Return (%)	Asset Value After Return ($)
1	50	10,000	33.1%	13,310
2	51	13,310	33.1%	17,716
3	52	17,716	33.1%	23,579
4	53	23,579	33.1%	31,384
5	54	31,384	33.1%	41,772
6	55	41,772	33.1%	55,599
7	56	55,599	33.1%	74,002
8	57	74,002	33.1%	98,497
9	58	98,497	33.1%	131,100
10	59	131,100	33.1%	174,494

Compound annual growth rate calculation:	
	$
Initial investment	10,000
End balance	174,494
Number of years	10
Compound rate of return	33.1%

The beauty of starting early in the above example, is that you are essentially letting time do its job. All you have to do is to start early, and pick the right economies, markets, and investments in which to invest. Remember, you have much greater control over the investment time horizon but much less control over the returns. Of course, you will have to keep an eye on the ETF and the market at large to make sure it continues its past trend.

Note too that investing in the equity markets tends to be more volatile. Given a longer time horizon, the high and the lows tend to smooth themselves out so that the average yields or losses will be much less extreme. So, if you start investing in the stock market with only two years to retirement, you may be trying to cash out the investment when the market is going through a recessionary period. This means that you will have no time to let it recover and take advantage of a rising market.

The point is: start early. If you start young, you have more time. If you start old, you have much less time. It does not matter how small your investment. A small tree will grow into a bigger tree. A big tree will grow into an even bigger tree. To wait till you have saved up enough before starting is misconceived, ill-advised, and runs counter to the best practice in investing.

Successful investing is also a matter of attitude. We often procrastinate because we are unconvinced since we have difficulty visualizing the result in the distant future. However, we should be able to work out the mathematical probability.

You may say 'I do not have $10k'.

1. If you are young, how about taking up a little side job, or live with your parents for a while before seeking independence.

2. How about starting with just a little seed money, maybe just $500, instead of $10k? If even that is too much, what about $100, or $50?

3. Invest as you earn. Try to earn a bit more, tighten your belt a bit more without too much pain, then invest every penny of it.

4. As a last resort you could humbly ask your parents to lend you some money. Your doting parents will always try and oblige!

The point is, try to start early.

If you are a parent, you want your children to have the funds for their college fees, or some savings to draw on during tough times. Start by investing. Start sowing the seed now for this emergency fund. A good start would be to put a sum, based on the dollar-cost averaging principle (see Chapter 15), into an index-tracking fund investing in a well-run market and leave it there for 20 years. I will explain this strategy later in the book but you can see the result in Illustration 5.

Times have changed; investing has never been easier. Investing and especially stock trading has been democratized in many parts of the world. With apps now online and ubiquitous, trading in many of the major markets of the world is at everyone's fingertips. With little or no trading commission at some brokerages, and the potential to buy even a fraction of a share, everyone can start investing (note: almost nothing in life is free, especially in the business world. Understand what you give up in return for a free trading fee).

Don't rely on the government. Don't envy the rich. Take responsibility for your finances. If your country's economy is not doing well, you may be able to lessen the adverse impact, at least financially, because your financial world is not limited to just your home country.

The point is, unless you are living from hand to mouth every day in a poverty-stricken country, everyone can start to invest. Once started, you will discover the way to participate in the success and prosperity of your country and the world. Investing can even be fun and exciting, especially once you begin to understand the financial markets and make money out of them.

Chapter 4
Earn More Than You Spend

Life is full of uncertainties and unforeseen circumstances; you don't need financial problems to add to them. It is said that money is the root of all evil – it can be, but it can also be used as a form of protection. In many Asian countries where the welfare system is much less than developed than in the western world, emergency medical bills often have to be assisted by loans from relatives and friends. Retirement expenses often have to be met by family members supporting each other. These are all the more reasons to be careful with money. You never know when the rainy days will come.

Earning without investing is living dangerously because emergencies can and probably will arise, out of nowhere, at some point in your life.

So, while still young and energetic, it is wise to make hay while the sun shines and save for the rainy days. Through the course of this long journey through life there will be many difficult days. It is important we have funds not just for ourselves but also to help out our loved ones when required. Everyone can save something, unless you are barely surviving every day. However, saving requires discipline. When discipline becomes a habit, the saving will be less burdensome.

Budgeting

Learn to budget. You have to know how much you are spending each month and each year and on what. There may be items on the list that surprise you. You did not know that they can add up very quickly. Some expenditure could be given up with little change to your lifestyle. See Illustration 2 – Income and expenses budget for a personal budgeting template on monthly income and expenses.

Illustration 2 – Income and expenses budget

Description	Monthly Budget	Month - Actual												
		1	2	3	4	5	6	7	8	9	10	11	12	YTD
Income ($)														
Salary	3,800	4,000	4,000											8,000
Rental income	-	500	500											1,000
Fixed deposit interest														-
Dividend received	100	200	100											300
Other	200	300	200											500
Total income	**4,100**	**5,000**	**4,800**	-	-	-	-	-	-	-	-	-	-	**9,800**
Expenses ($)														
Utility: power	500	400	500											900
Vehicle expenses														-
Groceries	1,000	2,000	2,300											4,300
Dining out	500	500	600											1,100
Mortgage payment														-
Taxes/rates/levy	50	100	100											200
Insurance														-
Other	200		300											300
Total expenses ($)	**2,250**	**3,000**	**3,800**	-	-	-	-	-	-	-	-	-	-	**6,800**
Income - Expenses	**1,850**	**2,000**	**1,000**	-	-	-	-	-	-	-	-	-	-	**3,000**

To achieve financial independence, we need to know what assets we own, and how many of these are investible assets, i.e. financial assets in which we have invested, excluding our primary residence. We own our primary residence to provide a roof over our heads. This contrasts with other investible assets which we invest in for the predominant objective of making a good return at an acceptable level of risk.

So, after we have secured a roof over our heads, we want to know how much we are saving each month and each year to invest in investible assets. For many people it is a matter of whatever loose change is left in the pocket at the end of the month after all our monthly expenditure. For others, the savings take different forms, some of which we may not even be aware. In reality, they include contributions into a retirement scheme (both the employee's and the employer's contribution); the employee stock purchases; auto deduction for health insurance type investment, etc. To omit any of them may lead to the wrong projection toward financial independence. Illustration 3, below, shows a consolidation of the various forms of savings.

Illustration 3 - Annual total savings

			$000/year
Description	**Employee Contribution**	**Employer Contribution**	**Total Savings**
401K retirement plan	4	2	6
Employee stocks purchase plan	1		1
Health saving plan	1		1
Monthly investment into ETFs	1		1
Savings (money left over from salary after above)	1		1
Total	**8**	**2**	**10**

The total amount of savings per year in the above illustration is $10k per year.

Your savings rate has a major impact on how soon you achieve financial independence. In Illustration 4 (below), if you put away an initial investment of $10k, with no extra annual saving hereafter at all, you will have an asset value of $174,494 at the end of year 30, assuming the rate of return is 10% per year, approximating the historical before tax return of the S&P. If this had been $30k instead of $10k, it would be $523,482 (before tax).

Illustration 4 – Summary of the effect of compounding

Investment period	Initial investment $		
	10,000	20,000	30,000
	Asset value (compounding)		
10 years	25,937	51,875	77,812
20 years	67,275	134,550	201,825
30 years	174,494	348,988	523,482
	Asset value (no compounding)		
10 years	20,000	40,000	60,000
20 years	30,000	60,000	90,000
30 years	40,000	80,000	120,000

Let's say in addition to the initial investment of $10k, you invest $1k, or $3k, or $5k per year for the next 30 years, the effects are seen in Illustration 6 - The effect of savings and compounding.

See Illustration 5 below for the summary. The asset value will be $338,988 at the end of 30 years. And if you increased the $1k to $5k per year ($417/month), at the end of 30 years, that becomes $996,964. This means if you start working at age 20 and start to save and invest, then, by age 50, you will have a cool million.

Illustration 5 - Summary of the effect of savings and compounding

Initial investment of $10k			
Investment Period	Asset Value ($)		
	Savings of $1,000	Savings of $3,000	Savings of $5,000
10 years	41,875	73,750	105,625
20 years	124,550	239,100	353,650
30 years	338,988	667,976	996,964

For many just starting out, this would still be a big ask. For others working in booming economies who have been gainfully employed for a number of years, the chances are that they can achieve even better results than this. They will have a bigger asset at the end and achieve financial independence even earlier.

Let me reiterate, the more disciplined you are, the more successful your investing will be. The more you earn, the more you spend, is not a good discipline, and not a good philosophy. Sure, it is permissible from time to time to pamper yourself a bit more as you earn more, but until you are secure, you do not want to overspend.

Illustration 6 - The effect of savings and compounding

Scenario assumptions: Initial investment $10K, savings invested $1K/$3K/$5K per year
Annual % return at 10%

Year	Starting Balance ($)	Investment Return (%)	Investment Balance After Return ($)	Savings $1K/year		Savings $3K/year		Savings $5K/year	
				Savings Put into Investment	Closing Balance	Savings Put into Investment	Closing Balance	Savings Put into Investment	Closing Balance
1	10,000	10%	11,000	1,000	12,000	3,000	14,000	5,000	16,000
2	12,000	10%	13,200	1,000	14,200	3,000	18,400	5,000	22,600
3	14,200	10%	15,620	1,000	16,620	3,000	23,240	5,000	29,860
4	16,620	10%	18,282	1,000	19,282	3,000	28,564	5,000	37,846
5	19,282	10%	21,210	1,000	22,210	3,000	34,420	5,000	46,631
6	22,210	10%	24,431	1,000	25,431	3,000	40,862	5,000	56,294
7	25,431	10%	27,974	1,000	28,974	3,000	47,949	5,000	66,923
8	28,974	10%	31,872	1,000	32,872	3,000	55,744	5,000	78,615
9	32,872	10%	36,159	1,000	37,159	3,000	64,318	5,000	91,477
10	37,159	10%	40,875	1,000	41,875	3,000	73,750	5,000	105,625
11	41,875	10%	46,062	1,000	47,062	3,000	84,125	5,000	121,187
12	47,062	10%	51,769	1,000	52,769	3,000	95,537	5,000	138,306
13	52,769	10%	58,045	1,000	59,045	3,000	108,091	5,000	157,136
14	59,045	10%	64,950	1,000	65,950	3,000	121,900	5,000	177,850
15	65,950	10%	72,545	1,000	73,545	3,000	137,090	5,000	200,635
16	73,545	10%	80,899	1,000	81,899	3,000	153,799	5,000	225,698
17	81,899	10%	90,089	1,000	91,089	3,000	172,179	5,000	253,268
18	91,089	10%	100,198	1,000	101,198	3,000	192,397	5,000	283,595
19	101,198	10%	111,318	1,000	112,318	3,000	214,636	5,000	316,955
20	112,318	10%	123,550	1,000	124,550	3,000	239,100	5,000	353,650
21	124,550	10%	137,005	1,000	138,005	3,000	266,010	5,000	394,015
22	138,005	10%	151,805	1,000	152,805	3,000	295,611	5,000	438,416
23	152,805	10%	168,086	1,000	169,086	3,000	328,172	5,000	487,258
24	169,086	10%	185,995	1,000	186,995	3,000	363,989	5,000	540,984
25	186,995	10%	205,694	1,000	206,694	3,000	403,388	5,000	600,082
26	206,694	10%	227,364	1,000	228,364	3,000	446,727	5,000	665,091
27	228,364	10%	251,200	1,000	252,200	3,000	494,400	5,000	736,600
28	252,200	10%	277,420	1,000	278,420	3,000	546,840	5,000	815,260
29	278,420	10%	306,262	1,000	307,262	3,000	604,524	5,000	901,786
30	307,262	10%	337,988	1,000	338,988	3,000	667,976	5,000	996,964

When your investments earn more than your spending each year, your asset base will continue to expand. You will then join the ranks of those we jealously call "the rich that get richer". For example, if you have accumulated investment assets of $1m and an average return could on average be 10% (for example, investing in equity market that tracks the broader US market, the S&P), then your annual investment income per year would be $100k. If your expenditure on average works out to be $40k, then there will still be $60k for re-investment. This means your assets will continue to grow.

On the other hand, if your income is only $100k but your expenditure is $200k, the deficit will have to be taken out of the $1m, which will shrink the asset base and hence its return in the coming years. If you are continuously eating into your principal, your investment will continue to shrink and the investment that you rely on as living expenses will also continue to shrink. There is no financial independence.

Discretionary Spending

Cancel or postpone expenditures that are not necessary if possible. Let's say you are young. You just landed your dream job. You have a girlfriend you want to impress. All your life you have dreamed of owning a sports car. You have the urge to spend $50k of your savings to fulfil your dream. See the two investment options you have with the $50k in the simplistic Illustration 7 below:

Illustration 7 - Discretionary spending (buying a car)

	Asset Value ($)
Savings used to buy a car:	
Cost of car	50,000
Depreciate for 5 years (10%/year*5=50%)	(25,000)
Net value of car after 5 years depreciation	25,000
Running cost and maintenance (assume nil as an offset against car/taxi rentals)	-
Asset value	**25,000**
Savings used to invest:	
Investment	50,000
Investment return per year	10%
*Asset value - investment value compounded after 5 years	**80,526**
Difference between buying car and return from investment	**55,526**

*Asset value - investment value compounded after 5 years:
($50,000*1.1*1.1*1.1*1.1*1.1)=$80,526

This comparison assumes the car buying is discretionary, i.e. you do not need it as a transportation tool. You can see the stark difference. Your wealth, in the form of a depreciated car, after 5 years is $25k. If this $50k was invested in an ETF tracking the S&P at 10% per year, by the end of year 5, the compounded asset value would be $80,526. The difference is $55,526. Imagine what the asset value will be if extended to 20 or 30 years. Why the vast difference? You are trying to enjoy something that loses value instead of using the cash to invest in something that is not only not losing value but is producing incremental value at a compounded rate. So, keep your urges in check, if you can help it. The more you save, the more the good money will generate effortless extra money for you in the years to come.

While this illustration uses car purchases as an example, this situation could easily arise many times over throughout your life. It could well involve the purchase of big-ticket discretionary items such as a boat, or a house renovation, or even an expensive hobby. Try not to let your ego cloud your thinking.

Chapter 5

Think Twice Before Taking on Debts

Incurring debt comes not only with a legal obligation but also a psychological burden. One cannot claim to be financially independent until one is debt-free because debts do have to be repaid. However, in real life, there are times when taking on debt may be necessary or even advantageous. Taking on debts may become necessary when the cash in hand is unable to overcome an emergency. Or there are compelling economic advantages in doing so; for example, taking out a loan at a very low interest rate of 2% for investment that is assured of preserving its value and a return of 10%. In real life though, nothing is for certain.

Taking on a debt, such as a loan, comes with obligations. Not only must you repay the principal, you also need to pay the interest owed, as contracted. Failure to do so could result in big losses, as any outstanding interest will continue to compound, to the point where a person could face bankruptcy.

For instance, a person could take out a mortgage loan to buy a property. If the mortgage cannot be serviced, the house may be disposed of, sometimes at a great loss, to settle the debt owed, including all outstanding interest. You can read more about the opportunity cost of buying versus renting a house in Chapter 9 - To buy or not to buy your own home.

Taking on debt comes with a commitment to repay when due. If the debt is too large that commitment can sometimes curtail a person's freedom and seriously affect a person's lifestyle. To be indebted to another person rather than a bank could even ruin a relationship.

It is sometimes tempting to borrow to keep up with a certain lifestyle. Many take up credit on their credit cards to pay for the luxuries they desire. The interest rates charged by credit card companies for the advance could be as high as 20% or more. If this is not repaid when due, penalty interest will be levied, not only on the outstanding interest but also on the unpaid penalty, on top of the already high credit card loan rate. Unchecked credit card debt can quickly escalate to overwhelm a person's finances.

This inability to repay the loans and debt obligations could affect your credit score. The credit score is a measure used in many countries to determine the creditworthiness of an individual. A poor credit score affects a person's ability to borrow from the banks, and credit extended by companies to their customers. It also affects the amount of the loan or credit and the cost of borrowing as the lender seeks to compensate themselves for the increased risk of defaults.

Even without considering the penalty, it does not make much economic sense to take up the credit card advance. If you have to use your card, repay it as soon as possible, preferably at the end of each month before you incur interest rate charges.

So, avoid the debt trap!

Chapter 6
The Significance of Investment as a Second Income Stream

From the beginning, we are fixated on getting an education and thereafter securing a career that sustains our livelihood. For many of us, our salary will always be the main source of income. We tend to ignore investment as an income stream which could make up a bigger and bigger proportion of our overall income in the course of our lives. The rich get richer because their money is working tirelessly for them, even though they have the same 24 hours in a day as you and me.

Not investing well means we may not have enough when we need it in the future, either because we have not saved enough, or because it has not made enough gains. Saving your surplus money in cash will not work because in most countries prices will rise over the years. If the inflation rate is 3% and the cash in the bank only yields 0.5%, when you retire in 30 years, the same amount of money will buy much less. So, as a simple goal, to start, we want to try to make an average return that beats the inflation rate and betters the alternative investment, in this case, the 0.5% on fixed-term deposit.

All investors should aim to optimize the gains from investment but with a big caveat - **without taking undue risk**. This is not just about money and about having the wealth to enjoy the things we dream of. It means much more. It could mean achieving freedom earlier, it could mean avoidance of misery, it means more years and better quality of life. With planning, discipline, and a good process, this is all within your grasp.

Based on Illustration 8 below, the summary is as follows: If you invest $10k at the beginning of year 1, and annually invest a further $5k, your asset will be worth $354k at end of year 20 and $997K at end of year 30.

Initial investment of $10k			
Investment Period	Asset Value ($)		
	Savings of $1,000	Savings of $3,000	Savings of $5,000
10 years	41,875	73,750	105,625
20 years	124,550	239,100	353,650
30 years	338,988	667,976	996,964

The investment income from this asset base from then on, at 10% return, will be $99.7k per year. If you start this process at age 20, by 50 you would have accumulated assets close to $1m, which will then give you about $100k per year before any capital gains tax. Is that enough to retire? At the very least, your prospect is a lot better than having to work till 65 and possibly beyond.

Income from investment

It is important to recognize very early on the importance of investment income in your overall financial well-being. We can only take up one full-time job, two at most, because everyone only has 24 hours in a day. We also need to take time to rest and enjoy ourselves. Fortunately, we are not the only ones who can make money. Money makes money! That's right, money begets money. With money, there is no limit. It works tirelessly, 24/7. The more you have, the more it will grow. Hence, the rich get richer; it's not their fault. And if this virtuous cycle is perpetuated through the next generation, it continues to get bigger and bigger.

Understanding this will benefit not just your generation but future ones as well. Look at it this way, regard your salary as the source of income that provides the seed money for investment and your sustenance from day to day. Investment is that extra that will turbocharge your finances. Your success in finance depends a lot on understanding it and being self-disciplined and much less on luck.

As the years go by, income from investment becomes more and more significant as a proportion of your overall income. If you succeed, you will reach an inflection point where it could even become the main income source. And all these things happen quietly while you slave away in the office. We always think of our jobs as the main source of our income. If we lose our jobs, our world would come crashing down. So we hold on to our jobs for dear life. We are enslaved by our jobs. We have to kowtow to our superiors lest our career is derailed. When you achieve financial independence you no longer have to beg for that annual salary increment or pray for that promotion.

The concept of an investment income for any household is important at so many levels. When you achieve income investment the income streams for the household lie not just those with jobs. You are no longer solely dependent on the job market and the economic success of a country. Because your investment income is diversified, the exposure is spread to provide hedging against downturns in different markets, sectors, and countries. It is the backup of a person, a family's finance in times of emergency.

If invested properly, for example, in ETFs, the investment is as good as emergency cash in times of need. It also provides a good hedge against inflation, as opposed to holding cash. Investors may also choose to buy stocks in companies that distribute dividends to their shareholders. These dividends are often distributed quarterly, providing regular income that may be required from time to time. Withdrawing from a retirement scheme prematurely often incurs penalties, but liquidating some investible assets of your own would be far more efficient and less costly.

Chapter 7

Max Out Subsidized Retirement Schemes

It is important you take an interest in this right from the beginning since it could well be the nest egg you rely on the most in retirement. It could also be the investment that gives you the best return in the long term. In the US, this could take the form of the 401K, in Malaysia it's called the EPF (Employee Providence Fund), and in Singapore the CPF (Central Provident Fund). Typically, employees contribute a certain percentage of their salary, subject to a limit, to be matched by their employers, which could be 50% or even more than the employee's contribution. So the retirement scheme will increase in its value with a contribution from the employee as well as the contribution from the employers, with annual returns on both contributions.

Let's simulate the common US retirement scheme 401K with a simple template - see Illustration 9. In this example, an employee's contribution of $10k per year is matched 50% by the employer/government. Given a 10% average annual return (as for S&P), the asset will be worth $263k in year 10, and $945k in year 20.

Illustration 9 – Retirement scheme returns

Assumptions: Employee contribution $10K/year, matched 50% by employer; 10% annual return

Year	Opening Balance	Employee Contribution	Employer Contribution	Cumulative Total	Investment Return (%)	*Investment Return ($)	Asset Value
1	0	10,000	5,000	15,000	10%	1,500	16,500
2	16,500	10,000	5,000	31,500	10%	3,150	34,650
3	34,650	10,000	5,000	49,650	10%	4,965	54,615
4	54,615	10,000	5,000	69,615	10%	6,962	76,577
5	76,577	10,000	5,000	91,577	10%	9,158	100,734
6	100,734	10,000	5,000	115,734	10%	11,573	127,308
7	127,308	10,000	5,000	142,308	10%	14,231	156,538
8	156,538	10,000	5,000	171,538	10%	17,154	188,692
9	188,692	10,000	5,000	203,692	10%	20,369	224,061
10	224,061	10,000	5,000	239,061	10%	23,906	262,968
11	262,968	10,000	5,000	277,968	10%	27,797	305,764
12	305,764	10,000	5,000	320,764	10%	32,076	352,841
13	352,841	10,000	5,000	367,841	10%	36,784	404,625
14	404,625	10,000	5,000	419,625	10%	41,962	461,587
15	461,587	10,000	5,000	476,587	10%	47,659	524,246
16	524,246	10,000	5,000	539,246	10%	53,925	593,171
17	593,171	10,000	5,000	608,171	10%	60,817	668,988
18	668,988	10,000	5,000	683,988	10%	68,399	752,386
19	752,386	10,000	5,000	767,386	10%	76,739	844,125
20	844,125	10,000	5,000	859,125	10%	85,912	945,037
Total		200,000	100,000			645,037	

*Assumed all contributions during the year received full year return.

Without the employer's contribution, this would only be worth $630,025 (see Illustration 10 below), i.e. 2/3 of the $945k.

Illustration 10 – Subsidized retirement scheme

Assumptions: Employee contribution $10K/year, matched 0% by employer; 10% annual return

Year	Opening Balance	Employee Contribution	Employer Contribution	Cumulative Total	Investment Return (%)	*Investment Return ($)	Asset Value
1	0	10,000	0	10,000	10%	1,000	11,000
2	11,000	10,000	0	21,000	10%	2,100	23,100
3	23,100	10,000	0	33,100	10%	3,310	36,410
4	36,410	10,000	0	46,410	10%	4,641	51,051
5	51,051	10,000	0	61,051	10%	6,105	67,156
6	67,156	10,000	0	77,156	10%	7,716	84,872
7	84,872	10,000	0	94,872	10%	9,487	104,359
8	104,359	10,000	0	114,359	10%	11,436	125,795
9	125,795	10,000	0	135,795	10%	13,579	149,374
10	149,374	10,000	0	159,374	10%	15,937	175,312
11	175,312	10,000	0	185,312	10%	18,531	203,843
12	203,843	10,000	0	213,843	10%	21,384	235,227
13	235,227	10,000	0	245,227	10%	24,523	269,750
14	269,750	10,000	0	279,750	10%	27,975	307,725
15	307,725	10,000	0	317,725	10%	31,772	349,497
16	349,497	10,000	0	359,497	10%	35,950	395,447
17	395,447	10,000	0	405,447	10%	40,545	445,992
18	445,992	10,000	0	455,992	10%	45,599	501,591
19	501,591	10,000	0	511,591	10%	51,159	562,750
20	562,750	10,000	0	572,750	10%	57,275	630,025
Total		200,000				430,025	

*Assumed all contributions during the year received full year return.

Not all countries and companies provide a subsidized retirement scheme. So be aware of what is available in your country and company. Understand how your company's scheme works. If the scheme allows participants to decide on the portfolio make-up, make sure you choose the portfolio best suited to your situation. For example, it would not be the best strategy to have a portfolio skewed towards fixed income if you are just starting and have an investment time horizon of at least 10-30 years. Instead, it should be skewed more to equity which has a higher return over the long term. There may also be other advantages associated with it. For example, the tax on the capital gains may be deferred until the fund is withdrawn.

Being a retirement scheme, on the other hand, there are also restrictions, such as penalties on early withdrawals.

In evaluating the financial package of a career or job offer, the financial benefits of the subsidized retirement scheme must be considered. Some jobs may have a less generous scheme, or you may even be ineligible for the scheme. For example, those self-employed, or working minimal hours, or on an extended time-off from work may not enjoy the most of the scheme. If one chooses not to work, one has to think ahead to the time when one will retire without the retirement payments.

Do not think that you are too young to think about retirement. The subsidized retirement scheme may be much more lucrative and significant than you think. Not bothering about it from the very beginning could mean that you end up not having enough to retire on. With many living a longer life, maximizing this asset will mean less worrying when you eventually come to retire.

Chapter 8

Take Advantage of Employee Stock Purchase Plans

In addition to paying their employees a salary, many public companies also offer company stock at a discount, as a staff incentive. This could work out to be a significant part of the salary package. So, whether you are looking for a new job or are already employed, be sure to take this into consideration and understand how it works.

The offers differ between countries and companies. For example, the offer may be offered every quarter subject to a limit; the discount rate could be 10% or more; there may be a lock-in period, etc. If you happen to be working for one of the high-growth companies, this asset could quickly accumulate significantly.

Let's use an illustration:

The young person's salary is $50k/year.

The company offers the company stock at a 15% discount every quarter, capped at 20% of the salary (i.e. $10k/year).

The company stock has been growing about 10%, consistently.

See the detailed calculation in Illustration 11 below:

Annual base salary	$50,000
Stock purchase entitlement capped at 20%	20%
Stock purchase	$10,000
Stock purchase at 15% discount	$8,500
Company stock price growth % per year	10%

Year	Starting Balance ($)	Investment Return %	Investment Balance After Return ($)	Employee stock purchase $10K/year		Employee stock purchase $8.5K/year	
				Savings Put into Investment	Closing Balance	Savings Put into Investment	Closing Balance
1	-	10%	-	10,000	10,000	8,500	8,500
2	10,000	10%	11,000	10,000	21,000	8,500	17,850
3	21,000	10%	23,100	10,000	33,100	8,500	28,135
4	33,100	10%	36,410	10,000	46,410	8,500	39,449
5	46,410	10%	51,051	10,000	61,051	8,500	51,893
6	61,051	10%	67,156	10,000	77,156	8,500	65,583
7	77,156	10%	84,872	10,000	94,872	8,500	80,641
8	94,872	10%	104,359	10,000	114,359	8,500	97,205
9	114,359	10%	125,795	10,000	135,795	8,500	115,426
10	135,795	10%	149,374	10,000	159,374	8,500	135,468
11	159,374	10%	175,312	10,000	185,312	8,500	157,515
12	185,312	10%	203,843	10,000	213,843	8,500	181,766
13	213,843	10%	235,227	10,000	245,227	8,500	208,443
14	245,227	10%	269,750	10,000	279,750	8,500	237,787
15	279,750	10%	307,725	10,000	317,725	8,500	270,066
16	317,725	10%	349,497	10,000	359,497	8,500	305,573
17	359,497	10%	395,447	10,000	405,447	8,500	344,630
18	405,447	10%	445,992	10,000	455,992	8,500	387,593
19	455,992	10%	501,591	10,000	511,591	8,500	434,852
20	511,591	10%	562,750	10,000	572,750	8,500	486,837
21	572,750	10%	630,025	10,000	640,025	8,500	544,021
22	640,025	10%	704,027	10,000	714,027	8,500	606,923
23	714,027	10%	785,430	10,000	795,430	8,500	676,116
24	795,430	10%	874,973	10,000	884,973	8,500	752,227
25	884,973	10%	973,471	10,000	983,471	8,500	835,950
26	983,471	10%	1,081,818	10,000	1,091,818	8,500	928,045
27	1,091,818	10%	1,200,999	10,000	1,210,999	8,500	1,029,350
28	1,210,999	10%	1,332,099	10,000	1,342,099	8,500	1,140,784
29	1,342,099	10%	1,476,309	10,000	1,486,309	8,500	1,263,363
30	1,486,309	10%	1,634,940	10,000	1,644,940	8,500	1,398,199

Note: Assumed stock purchased during the year will only start to receive return the following year.

See Illustration 12 below for the summary:

Investment Period	Asset Value at End of The Investment Period ($)	
	Annual stock purchase with discount ($10K)	Annual stock purchase without discount ($8.5K)
10 years	159,374	135,468
20 years	572,750	486,837
30 years	1,634,940	1,398,199

So, if the employee continues to take advantage of the employee stock purchase plan offered by the company, and with the company on average growing at 10% per year, the asset value at the end of years 10, 20, and 30 would be worth $159k, $572k, and $1.6m respectively. If the shares were purchased at market value, i.e. without the benefit of the discount of 15% offered, it would be worth only $135k, $486k, and $1.4m in years 10, 20, and 30 respectively.

So what looks like a small aspect of one's salary package could become very significant because the employee chose to work for a company that not only offers employee stock purchase at regular intervals and at a generous discount but also a company growing at a phenomenal rate.

This assumption may seem far-fetched but it really isn't. In today's technological environment, many companies are in fact enjoying very high growth rates (see Illustration 13 below - Big Tech past performances) and do offer such incentives.

Compound Annual Growth Rates					
No. of years	Microsoft	Amazon	Apple	Facebook	Google
1	37%	30%	56%	43%	65%
2	43%	36%	70%	36%	46%
3	37%	26%	40%	19%	28%
5	37%	35%	39%	23%	26%
Market Cap	1.9T	1.6T	2.1T	932b	816b

Note: The data above was extracted during the time of the writing and could have since changed. The table is for reference and illustrative purposes only. Any purchasing of the products should refer to the latest official documents.

Note: The annualized return above will change depending on the periods covered.

This is to remind you not to underestimate the potential contribution of this scheme. Unless you think the company has poor prospects and its share prices can only decline, do take a closer look at your employee stock purchase scheme.

Though this is the company one works for and which you are most likely to understand in depth, there is still a need to regularly rebalance and diversify the holding, lest it becomes too overweight in your overall investment portfolio.

Chapter 9

To Buy or Not To Buy Your Own Home

Buying a house is probably the biggest purchase you will ever make. Buying a home could be a lifelong venture that will change your finances forever. Do the calculations carefully before you take the plunge.

Owning your own home brings the feeling of 'home sweet home' that renting is unlikely to give. In many countries where property prices continue to skyrocket, home ownership provides the security and the prospect of capital gains but also presents financial challenges. In China, for example, house prices, especially in the big cities, have skyrocketed since its opening up, making homeowners a fortune, and those not owning it living in an ever-remoter dream. Buying property is also popular in some markets due to limited alternative investment opportunities. For example, property may provide some returns even if a country's stock market has not been performing well.

On the other hand, with such a big part of one's assets tied up in a house, it can also be a big risk. One could buy a property that not only may not appreciate but could actually depreciate. It could mean forgoing other more lucrative investment opportunities. If a big loan is taken up to finance the purchase, there will be the additional burden of interest and principal repayments over many years. If the property were to lose its value, to a below-market valuation, the lending institutions may even recall the loan and the property could then be lost to the owner.

In addition, there can be other concerns associated with owning a property. The constant worry of rising interest rates, the loss of one's earning power during this long period, etc. You are also at the mercy of your employer as you try to keep your job; you are at the mercy of the bank not to raise rates; you are at the mercy of the housing market, hoping that the property prices will hold up and appreciate; you are at the mercy of everything around you so that you can live up to the commitment of the loan agreement. There are so many uncertainties. There is little wriggle room. There is the constant psychological burden. This is not financial freedom. You can become enslaved by the house.

When forced to sell, a home is almost always more illiquid than other investments such as stock holdings. The sale of a house involves legal, administrative, tax, and a whole host of personal issues to settle, all of which take time to settle before the proceeds are received. Disposing of the house in the event of a small urgent cash need seems almost too costly. Of course, one could take up a loan against the value of the house but this again involves taking up a loan and its servicing. In contrast, company stocks are a lot more liquid and the process much simpler.

So owning a property could derail your plan towards financial independence. It could mean you may never achieve financial freedom. It could mean that your children would also have to start anew, just like you.

This is the fundamental problem with being in debt, especially when it is highly leveraged. Debt has to be repaid, or you face the significant consequences of non-repayment. Such are the realities of life.

This is not to say that one should not ever consider buying one's own home. Everyone deserves their castle. The question is: are you taking on something that you may not be ready to enjoy? Taking up a loan to purchase a home is essentially borrowing to enjoy something you are not yet able to afford and borrowing to invest in something (one big all-in investment) thinking it will provide positive returns in the long term. Sure, investing in one's own home is not the same as other investments; it serves a dual purpose - if it does not work as an investment, it is still one's home. Everyone needs a home.

Can you afford to buy a house?

Buying your own home may be less risky if:

- you have the cash to do so and there are no foreseeable better alternative investment opportunities

- you only take up a small loan so you can repay in a short time, your exposure to those uncertain factors would be much less

- the property prices are almost certain to rise significantly in the long term to make it worthwhile to forego other investment opportunities and the risks of taking up a big loan.

If the situation is still not clear, then rent for a while until the situation becomes clearer. Meantime, save up or invest until you have a high enough deposit for the house you want, thereby reducing your leverage.

So then, how do we decide which is the best option?

Let's try to quantify the financial impact of each of the buy or rent options, with a simple example of a small apartment purchase in Malaysia.

This is the annual budget of the potential buyer (Illustration 14):

Rent Option:	
Salary per year	$50,000
Living expenses per year	$36,000
Rental/year (assumed 5% of property price), instead of owning	$5,000
Money available for investment (salary - living expenses - rental)	$9,000

Buy Option:	
Property cost	$100,000
Own cash put down as house deposit	$20,000
Loan	$80,000
Mortgage interest rate (on loan balance end of period)	5%
Mortgage interest (year 1)	$4,000
Loan duration (years)	20
Loan repayment per year	$4,000
Money available for investment (salary - living expenses - rental - loan repayment)	$6,000

Investment asset value at end of year 20 with the rent option (Illustration 15):

| Asset Value - Rent Instead of Buying Own Home | | | | | | | | $ |
Year	Own Cash	Salary	Living Expenses	Rental	*Money Available for Investment	Asset at Year End	Invest in VOO	Investment Returns ($)	Asset Value at Year End
1	20,000	50,000	36,000	5,000	29,000	29,000	10%	2,900	31,900
2		50,000	36,000	5,000	9,000	40,900	10%	4,090	44,990
3		50,000	36,000	5,000	9,000	53,990	10%	5,399	59,389
4		50,000	36,000	5,000	9,000	68,389	10%	6,839	75,228
5		50,000	36,000	5,000	9,000	84,228	10%	8,423	92,651
6		50,000	36,000	5,000	9,000	101,651	10%	10,165	111,816
7		50,000	36,000	5,000	9,000	120,816	10%	12,082	132,897
8		50,000	36,000	5,000	9,000	141,897	10%	14,190	156,087
9		50,000	36,000	5,000	9,000	165,087	10%	16,509	181,596
10		50,000	36,000	5,000	9,000	190,596	10%	19,060	209,655
11		50,000	36,000	5,000	9,000	218,655	10%	21,866	240,521
12		50,000	36,000	5,000	9,000	249,521	10%	24,952	274,473
13		50,000	36,000	5,000	9,000	283,473	10%	28,347	311,820
14		50,000	36,000	5,000	9,000	320,820	10%	32,082	352,902
15		50,000	36,000	5,000	9,000	361,902	10%	36,190	398,093
16		50,000	36,000	5,000	9,000	407,093	10%	40,709	447,802
17		50,000	36,000	5,000	9,000	456,802	10%	45,680	502,482
18		50,000	36,000	5,000	9,000	511,482	10%	51,148	562,630
19		50,000	36,000	5,000	9,000	571,630	10%	57,163	628,793
20		50,000	36,000	5,000	9,000	637,793	10%	63,779	701,572

*Money available for investment: salary, living expenses, rental.

Note:
1) Assumed no salary adjustments, similarly no inflation on living expenses and rentals.
2) Assumed new investment during the year received full year return.

Total assets - investment asset at end of 20 years	701,572

Investment asset value at end of year 20 with the buy option (Illustration 16):

Asset Value - Buy Instead of Rent

Year	Loan	Interest Rate	Loan Interest	Loan Repayment	Salary	Living Expenses	*Money Available for Investment	Asset at Year End	Invest in VOO	Investment Returns	$ Investment Value at Year End
1	80,000	5%	4,000	4,000	50,000	36,000	6,000	6,000	10%	600	6,600
2	76,000	5%	3,800	4,000	50,000	36,000	6,200	12,800	10%	1,280	14,080
3	72,000	5%	3,600	4,000	50,000	36,000	6,400	20,480	10%	2,048	22,528
4	68,000	5%	3,400	4,000	50,000	36,000	6,600	29,128	10%	2,913	32,041
5	64,000	5%	3,200	4,000	50,000	36,000	6,800	38,841	10%	3,884	42,725
6	60,000	5%	3,000	4,000	50,000	36,000	7,000	49,725	10%	4,972	54,697
7	56,000	5%	2,800	4,000	50,000	36,000	7,200	61,897	10%	6,190	68,087
8	52,000	5%	2,600	4,000	50,000	36,000	7,400	75,487	10%	7,549	83,036
9	48,000	5%	2,400	4,000	50,000	36,000	7,600	90,636	10%	9,064	99,699
10	44,000	5%	2,200	4,000	50,000	36,000	7,800	107,499	10%	10,750	118,249
11	40,000	5%	2,000	4,000	50,000	36,000	8,000	126,249	10%	12,625	138,874
12	36,000	5%	1,800	4,000	50,000	36,000	8,200	147,074	10%	14,707	161,782
13	32,000	5%	1,600	4,000	50,000	36,000	8,400	170,182	10%	17,018	187,200
14	28,000	5%	1,400	4,000	50,000	36,000	8,600	195,800	10%	19,580	215,380
15	24,000	5%	1,200	4,000	50,000	36,000	8,800	224,180	10%	22,418	246,598
16	20,000	5%	1,000	4,000	50,000	36,000	9,000	255,598	10%	25,560	281,158
17	16,000	5%	800	4,000	50,000	36,000	9,200	290,358	10%	29,036	319,393
18	12,000	5%	600	4,000	50,000	36,000	9,400	328,793	10%	32,879	361,673
19	8,000	5%	400	4,000	50,000	36,000	9,600	371,273	10%	37,127	408,400
20	4,000	5%	200	4,000	50,000	36,000	9,800	418,200	10%	41,820	460,020

*Money available for investment: salary, living expenses, rental.
Note:
1) Assumed no salary adjustments, similarly no inflation on living expenses and rentals.
2) Assumed new investment during the year received full year return.

The total value of investment assets at end of year 20 is $460,020.

The financial comparison between the rent and buy option is as follows:

Difference in asset value at the end of year 20:	
Buy own home - Investment asset value (savings to invest after paying mortgages)	$460,020
Rent home - Total asset value (from next table)	$701,572
Value of the property, in order to match the rental option below	$241,552
Value of the house has to increase by (over 20 years) i.e. ($241,552-100,000)/100,000*100%	142%

Rent option

- value of investment assets at end of year 20 ($701,572)

Buy option

- value of investment assets + and value of the house, at end of year 20

- $460,020 + (purchase cost of the house + capital gains on the house over 20 years).

   To match the return on the buy option, the house will have to be worth $241,552 ($701,572 - $460,020), Which means the capital gains on the house over the 20 years will have to be $141,552 (i.e. $241,552 - $100,000). This means the house will have to appreciate by 141.5%.

   With $20k in cash and savings per year of $9k to invest in S&P tracking ETF (e.g. VOO) for an average 10% return, the wealth at the end of year 20 will be $701,572. If you were to buy a home, with a cash down payment of $20k and taking an $80k loan for a property priced at $100k, you would save on home rental but instead pay an interest rate of 5% and loan principal over 20 years. This option results in an investment worth $460,020 and a house at the end of 20 years. The house would have to be worth $241,552 to match the rent option, which is an increase in value of $141,552 (from the purchase price of $100k), or 141.5% over 20 years. This comparison ignores the capital gains tax, the depreciation in the house value after 20 years, and the cost of house maintenance over the 20 years.

   A property price increase of 141.5% over 20 years may not sound like too much to expect, however, in some countries, due to government measures, like ownership restrictions, price control, and tax burden, home capital gains would be more limited.

The illustration is simplistic and for illustrative purposes only. Any change in any of the parameters in the illustration could drastically alter the result. It should not be used for all cases in all countries and all circumstances, and certainly not as an argument for or against buying your own home. It does, however, present and highlight the many aspects of this difficult decision; it urges you to do the calculations and to weigh all the qualitative and quantitative factors.

If you do decide to take out a loan to buy a home, repaying the loan as quickly as possible is an option worth considering. You would save on the interest payment, which is serviced by your hard-earned after-tax money. Secondly, the saving on the interest payment may offer a good return. For example, if the loan interest is as high as 8%, this would be equivalent to an investment return of 8% after tax. That is an investment not easy to achieve otherwise. There are of course times when keeping the loan is a good option e.g. in the case where interest payment is tax-deductible, or the interest rate has been consistently almost negligible.

You may want to put your urge to buy on hold for a while you are young, unsettled, and uncertain about your career. Stay with your parents for a while longer, or maybe rent a room. When you are ready, and if you must buy, perhaps buy a small property to start with so that you have more disposable cash and only a small loan. Remember the principle of keeping life simple. If there are too many complications, you should choose the option with the least uncertainty. Life is full of unpleasant surprises, you don't need things to be exacerbated by running out of money.

If you are in the happy position of being able to buy a residential property as an investment, do weigh the pluses and minuses. In some countries and cultures, including many in Asia, investing in property has traditionally been popular. After all, bricks and mortar are tangible; something we can better understand and therefore perceived to be better as an asset preservation. In many cases, it is also due to the lack of investment alternatives.

However, for retail investors, many aspects of this investment must be considered. For one, property investment is quite a concentrated bet, often of a sizeable amount relative to one's overall portfolio and in one sector, i.e. the property sector.

Let's look at a situation for illustrative purposes:

A property owner in Malaysia puts all of their savings into a few well-located properties, as opposed to investing in other investments, for example, the stock market. The property market in the country has been pretty depressed for the last few years. The rental rates have been declining. Property values have remained stagnant and maybe even declined. The situation has been made much worst in the past 18 months by Covid-19. Some of the properties remain vacant because the economy has been bad. The expat market has been decimated because no one can come into the country. Meantime, the related major expenses such as management fees, sinking fund, insurance and land dues continue to be payable.

Let's demonstrate with an example how problematic this investment could be, should the property market be unfavourable.

For an apartment of RM1m in Kuala Lumpur, the market rental is RM3,500/month for a fully furnished apartment in the city centre. Expats typically rent for a year and sometimes renew for another six months or a year. The owner pays the equivalent of one month agency fee plus 6% tax to the estate agents for securing the tenants. The new tenants would typically request the replacement of some items like furniture, TV, electricals, etc., or a reduced rental before moving in.

After the lease expiry, there would typically be a vacant period of at least one month because agents do not normally start working on the property again until the previous tenants have vacated the premises. When prospective tenants have indicated interest, their earliest move-in date will typically be in two weeks.

After the first year, should the tenants decide to extend the lease, it is more than likely that they would ask for better terms, including reduced rental, and maybe more household content to be added, knowing that the owner will have to incur even more costs in placing new tenants (another month of agency fees and enduring another potential vacant period and more demands from the new tenants). The owner bears the management fee of about RM8k per year, plus land dues of RM2k.

When the tenants finally move out, a lot of chores are required of the owner. Inspection has to be done, inventory taken, damaged items repaired or replaced; air conditioners serviced; curtains and sofa laundered. Most of these are usually charged at the owners' expense. Then the hard job of looking for new tenants and negotiations begins; along with the administrative work of the agency agreement and tenancy agreement; and the arrangement for the move-in of the new tenants.

See table below:

Illustration 17 – Property investment return

Description	Rm$/year
Rental income	38,500
Less: Expenses	
Agency fee	3,710
Management fee	8,000
Land dues	1,500
Repairs and replacement	2,000
Net income	23,290
Property cost and market value	1,000,000
Return on investment	2.3%

At the end of the year, the owner adds up all the rental income and deducts the expenses. They will also have to pay personal income tax on the income received from the property.

If the owner has a few of these properties, they may well be overwhelmed by the work involved in managing them. So in many situations the odds can be pretty well stacked against the owner, the investor of the property. In situations where available capital is an issue, this outsized investment requires a rethink.

The real estate market may be better in some countries than others, but in the above scenario, it is a lot of work for minuscule returns. There are simply too many potential downsides; this is not a good investment. So, do the maths, weigh the pluses and the minuses carefully before considering property as an investment.

Chapter 10
The Effect of Compounding

When the returns from an investment are re-invested, it generates a return on the investment. The return will get bigger each year during the period of profitability. This is the snowballing effect that over years, will expedite the growth of the asset. That is, not only will the initial money you put in make money, the money that it makes will also itself make money.

Expressed mathematically, compounding an annual 10% return on a principal of $100 over 3 years is $10*110%*110%*110%=$133.10. A simple average is $10+($10*10%*3 years) =$130. If maths is not your thing, let's try it another way.

If you start off with 100 geese, by the end of year one, you should have 110 geese because your return is 10%. Starting year two, you now have 110 geese working to produce more geese at the same rate, i.e. 10%, so that at the end of year 2, you will get 121 geese (not just 120). You start off year 3 with 121 geese producing more geese. By end of year 3, you now have 133 geese, and so on and so forth. This is because the geese producing geese are themselves producing new geese at the same rate.

For example, if $10k, or $20k, or $30k is invested in the S&P, see the snowballing effect of compounding in Illustration 18

Illustration 18 – The effect of compounding

Scenario assumptions: Investment amount $10K/$20K/$30K, investment return 10%/year

	Initial Investment $10K			Initial Investment $20K		Initial Investment $30K	
Year	Starting Balance ($)	Investment Return %	Investment Balance Plus Return ($)	Starting Balance ($)	Investment Balance Plus Return ($)	Starting Balance ($)	Investment Balance Plus Return ($)
1	10,000	10%	11,000	20,000	22,000	30,000	33,000
2	11,000	10%	12,100	22,000	24,200	33,000	36,300
3	12,100	10%	13,310	24,200	26,620	36,300	39,930
4	13,310	10%	14,641	26,620	29,282	39,930	43,923
5	14,641	10%	16,105	29,282	32,210	43,923	48,315
6	16,105	10%	17,716	32,210	35,431	48,315	53,147
7	17,716	10%	19,487	35,431	38,974	53,147	58,462
8	19,487	10%	21,436	38,974	42,872	58,462	64,308
9	21,436	10%	23,579	42,872	47,159	64,308	70,738
10	23,579	10%	25,937	47,159	51,875	70,738	77,812
11	25,937	10%	28,531	51,875	57,062	77,812	85,594
12	28,531	10%	31,384	57,062	62,769	85,594	94,153
13	31,384	10%	34,523	62,769	69,045	94,153	103,568
14	34,523	10%	37,975	69,045	75,950	103,568	113,925
15	37,975	10%	41,772	75,950	83,545	113,925	125,317
16	41,772	10%	45,950	83,545	91,899	125,317	137,849
17	45,950	10%	50,545	91,899	101,089	137,849	151,634
18	50,545	10%	55,599	101,089	111,198	151,634	166,798
19	55,599	10%	61,159	111,198	122,318	166,798	183,477
20	61,159	10%	67,275	122,318	134,550	183,477	201,825
21	67,275	10%	74,002	134,550	148,005	201,825	222,007
22	74,002	10%	81,403	148,005	162,805	222,007	244,208
23	81,403	10%	89,543	162,805	179,086	244,208	268,629
24	89,543	10%	98,497	179,086	196,995	268,629	295,492
25	98,497	10%	108,347	196,995	216,694	295,492	325,041
26	108,347	10%	119,182	216,694	238,364	325,041	357,545
27	119,182	10%	131,100	238,364	262,200	357,545	393,300
28	131,100	10%	144,210	262,200	288,420	393,300	432,630
29	144,210	10%	158,631	288,420	317,262	432,630	475,893
30	158,631	10%	174,494	317,262	348,988	475,893	523,482

Compound annual growth rate calculation:			
	$	$	$
Initial investment	10,000	20,000	30,000
End balance	174,494	348,988	523,482
Number of years	30	30	30
Compound rate of return	10.0%	10.0%	10.0%

The table below summarizes the effects:

Illustration 19:

Investment Period	Initial Investment ($)		
	10,000	20,000	30,000
	Asset Value (Compounding)		
10 years	25,937	51,875	77,812
20 years	67,275	134,550	201,825
30 years	174,494	348,988	523,482
	Asset Value (No Compounding)		
10 years	20,000	40,000	60,000
20 years	30,000	60,000	90,000
30 years	40,000	80,000	120,000

Note: No tax effects have been considered above.

The bigger the investment, the greater the returns; the longer the time horizon, the greater the result. For example, $20k invested for 20 years will end up having a value of $134,550, as opposed to $60k without compounding; if $30k is invested over 30 years, it will be worth $523,482 in contrast to $120k with no compounding.

The investment does not have to be limited to 30 years. Let's say you are now 30 and starting to be worried about your old age. So you start looking ahead 30 years to when you are 60. Or maybe you are worried about your children. You want to make sure they have some kind of nest egg when they retire. So your investment time horizon, in this case, is not just 30 years; it could be as long as 80 - 90 years. Guess what putting a sum of money over 80 - 90 years will produce if you let compounding work its magic?

If we plug the 80 years investment horizon, the result will be as shown in the table below.

Illustration 20 – The effect of compounding, extended to 80 years.

Scenario assumptions: Investment amount $10K/$20K/$30K, investment return 10%/year

| | Initial Investment $10K | | | Initial Investment $20K | | Initial Investment $30K | |
Year	Starting Balance ($)	Investment Return %	Investment Balance Plus Return ($)	Starting Balance ($)	Investment Balance Plus Return ($)	Starting Balance ($)	Investment Balance Plus Return ($)
1	10,000	10%	11,000	20,000	22,000	30,000	33,000
2	11,000	10%	12,100	22,000	24,200	33,000	36,300
3	12,100	10%	13,310	24,200	26,620	36,300	39,930
4	13,310	10%	14,641	26,620	29,282	39,930	43,923
5	14,641	10%	16,105	29,282	32,210	43,923	48,315
6	16,105	10%	17,716	32,210	35,431	48,315	53,147
7	17,716	10%	19,487	35,431	38,974	53,147	58,462
8	19,487	10%	21,436	38,974	42,872	58,462	64,308
9	21,436	10%	23,579	42,872	47,159	64,308	70,738
10	23,579	10%	25,937	47,159	51,875	70,738	77,812
11	25,937	10%	28,531	51,875	57,062	77,812	85,594
12	28,531	10%	31,384	57,062	62,769	85,594	94,153
13	31,384	10%	34,523	62,769	69,045	94,153	103,568
14	34,523	10%	37,975	69,045	75,950	103,568	113,925
15	37,975	10%	41,772	75,950	83,545	113,925	125,317
16	41,772	10%	45,950	83,545	91,899	125,317	137,849
17	45,950	10%	50,545	91,899	101,089	137,849	151,634
18	50,545	10%	55,599	101,089	111,198	151,634	166,798
19	55,599	10%	61,159	111,198	122,318	166,798	183,477
20	61,159	10%	67,275	122,318	134,550	183,477	201,825
30	158,631	10%	174,494	317,262	348,988	475,893	523,482
80	18,621,820	10%	20,484,002	37,243,640	40,968,004	55,865,460	61,452,006

Compound annual growth rate calculation:			
	$	$	$
Initial investment	10,000	20,000	30,000
End balance	20,484,002	40,968,004	61,452,006
Number of years	80	80	80
Compound rate of return	10.0%	10.0%	10.0%

This effect is summarized below:

Illustration 21 – Summary of the effect of compounding, extended to 80 years.

Asset Value at End of	Initial Investment		
	10,000	20,000	30,000
10 years	25,937	51,875	77,812
20 years	67,275	134,550	201,825
30 years	174,494	348,988	523,482
80 years	20,484,002	40,968,004	61,452,006

After 80 years, 10k invested becomes $20.4m; $20k becomes $41m; $30k becomes $61.5m.

The beauty of passive investing is that you do not have to do much; it does not have to consume much of your time. As you work away at the office your investment is quietly working and accumulating for you. All you have to do is:

1. come up with the initial savings for investment - the more the merrier

2. resist the temptation to spend the annual returns

3. invest in markets that have positive earnings growth over time (example US S&P)

4. monitor the market/country/economy to ensure that they do not change unfavourably. Drastic political, demographic, or other economic structure changes will affect the share price of companies in that country (see also Chapter 18 - The Macro Picture).

The tax effects from capital gains and other taxes have not been factored in here (see Chapter 17 - Tax Matters). Taxes vary between countries. For example, some countries impose capital gains tax while others do not.

Chapter 11

Understanding Major Investment Types

There are a wide variety of investment instruments on the market, ranging from the basic to the extremely exotic. For the retail investor just starting out, let's look at the more commonly available ones.

Let's first identify the major types of instruments before we narrow in on the specific products. The common ones are bonds, mutual funds, exchange-traded funds (ETFs), and individual company stocks, also called shares. All of these are available in most countries.

Mutual fund

This is an investment fund consisting of securities (stocks, bonds, etc) managed by professional fund managers, using funds pooled from investors. This is usually actively managed by the fund managers, i.e. professional investors who buy and sell securities as they see fit. In return, they charge a management fee of up to and above 1% on the asset. They usually also charge a one-time cost of 1-5% to buy-in. It is an easy way to invest, for those who have little investing knowledge and who prefer to have their investments handled by professionals.

The most important factors to consider before buying into a mutual fund are:

- the fund strategy

- the one-time buy-in fee

- the fund fee

- past performance of the fund

- reputation of the fund company.

It is important to pick funds with a fund strategy that meets your performance expectation. The strategy may be to focus on a particular country (e.g. China, US, India); a region (e.g. Europe, Asia); a sector (e.g. IT, Finance, Healthcare); or themes (e.g. clean energy, space).

Mutual funds are usually held for a longer time horizon. The one-time buy-in fee makes that almost necessary. So, picking the right fund from the beginning is important. After the buy-in, it is important to monitor performance. As much as you would like to trust the capability of the fund managers, if they do not perform, cut your losses and move on.

Exchange Traded Fund (ETF)

An exchange-traded fund (ETF) is a type of security that is traded on the exchange, much like a stock. It consists of a basket of securities that are selected to reflect the overall performance of the sector in which it operates. Like mutual funds, its strategy could involve tracking an index, an industry sector, or geography.

The most obvious advantage is the low expense ratio, which is almost negligible. This lower fee is possible because most ETFs are passively managed. In contrast, mutual funds could charge anything from 0.5% to 1% for active management. But isn't active management supposed to produce better results? In many cases, active investment managers are not able to pick enough winners to justify their high fees. Although some managers succeed in beating the market, few can repeat it consistently. In trying to beat the market, fund managers might engage in frequent buying and selling, triggering unnecessary capital gains tax for example. When their higher expenses are charged over a long period, in profitable as well as loss-making years, the impact can be significant (see Chapter 16 – Expenses Matter).

This form of investment has become very popular in the past two decades with assets totaling in the trillions. It has become one of the key investment vehicles used by financial professionals in managing money for their clients. As an investor, first, understand what an ETF is and how it works. Then decide in what ETF you would like to invest - geography, industry sector, theme, etc.

If you are unsure, then simply pick a fund that covers an entire stock market. As long as the overall stock market rises, so will the shares that you have invested via your ETF. For example, you may want to look at an ETF that tracks the S&P 500. This fund invests in *all* of the top 500 companies in America.

Go to your brokerage platform (for example Charles Schwab) and using the screen options, define the various criteria desired – size, inception, expense ratio, fund houses, returns, dividends, sector etc. Before placing the order, be sure to read up the strategy statement to make sure it matches your expectation. A policy statement that says "*The investment seeks to track the performance of the Standard & Poor's 500 Index and investing all, or substantially all, of its assets in the stocks that make up the index, holding each stock in approximately the same proportion as its weighting in the index...*" may be suitable if you are looking to invest in the broader US stock market. See Illustration 22 below on such ETFs (ticker symbols VOO and IVV) that meet the criteria. These are the larger ETFs that have years of track record, are low expense, and are administered by reputable fund houses.

Illustration 22

Description	ETF	
	VOO	**IVV**
Expenses ratio	0.03%	0.03%
Size	731b	278b
Inception - year	2010	2000
Fund company	Vanguard	Blackrock
Distributing/Accumulative	Distributing	Distributing
Dividend yield	1.40%	1.36%
Performance:		
1 year	56%	56%
5 years	16%	16%
10 years	14%	14%
Since inception	15%	7%
Top 10 holdings and %:	(See if the holdings reflect the strategy you have in mind)	
Strategy	Seeks to track the performance of the S&P500	Seeks to track the performance of the S&P500

Note 1:
Distributing is funds that distribute dividends to its investors. Accumulating is funds that reinvest the investor's dividends within the fund

Note 2:
The data above was extracted during the time of the writing and could have since changed. The table is for reference and illustrative purposes only. Any purchasing of the products should refer to the latest official documents.

Perhaps the biggest advantage of an ETF is that it is real-time and transparent, relative to mutual funds. Because ETFs are traded like a stock on the exchanges, one can buy and sell in response to the up-to-the-second information. So, if the channels are reporting breaking news that will impact the market, and the S&P is reacting to it, you could expect the ETF which tracks the S&P (example VOO) to change more or less to the same extent.

In contrast, because the underlying stock holding of a mutual fund is at the discretion of the fund managers, it is not as transparent, and not so real-time. So, when an order is placed with your fund managers, the exact price transacted is not known until it is finally completed. In today's volatile market, with so many fast-changing factors and events, this difference is critical.

The ETF has come a long way. There are now a huge range of sectors or themes in which one can investing. For example, if you fancy betting on China IT, you could buy CQQQ. Or if you fancy the healthcare sector in the US, you could buy VHT.

Not all ETFs are passively managed. There are now ETFs that are actively managed. This would be suitable for investors looking for fund managers actively identifying opportunities, especially in a market conducive to active stock picking, yet unlike a mutual fund, one which is tradeable, more transparent, and real-time. An example would be the ARK ETFs (example ARKK/ARKW/ARKG/ARKF) with fund managers actively looking for opportunities in the disruptive technology area which retail investors would otherwise not be able to do themselves. Other examples of active ETFs are the Dimension ETFs.

For those looking for non-US domiciled ETFs, quite often for tax reasons, try to search for them on Justetf.com.

Domicile is where you are permanently resident. A fund also has a domicile, i.e. where the fund's holding company is incorporated, and therefore usually also where the management of the fund is located. A fund may be domiciled in the US but invest in companies situated outside the US. Where you are domiciled affects how you are taxed on the investment. Where the fund you invest in is domiciled also affects how you are taxed on the investment.

For example, if a US tax resident invests in VOO - a US domiciled ETF tracking the S&P - and receives a dividend from it, they will be charged a dividend tax according to the local tax rate applicable at the time. If a foreigner, let's say, a Malaysian, were to buy the same ETF (VOO), the same dividend will be taxed at 30% by the US Tax Department. If they were to buy a similar ETF (for example with the ticker symbol VUSD) that tracks the S&P, this fund is domiciled in Ireland instead of the US, and so the tax rate by the US tax department will only be at 15%. Of course, tax is not the only consideration when deciding where a fund is domiciled. Other factors, like the size of the fund and the management expenses are also important factors. Also see Chapter 17 on Tax Matters.

Company stocks

Buying the stock of a company is potentially riskier than buying a mutual fund or ETF which holds hundreds of stocks. A company's performance could be impacted by many factors, some unforeseen and beyond its control. Some companies are less risky than others, especially if they are bigger, financially well cashed, have a big moat to discourage new competition, have multi-stream income, are innovative, and have a long track record of performance, etc. These companies are called 'blue-chip stocks'.

Still, a company's fortune could change from day to day, its stock price could skyrocket in a short time, but it could also drop to nil in an extreme case; for example, Enron and Lehman Brothers. There are ways, however, to mitigate the risks. For more details on this see Chapter 19 - The Art and Science of Stock Picking .

Bonds

Instead of investing in equity, one could invest in fixed income, also called bonds. Bonds are a kind of I.O.U issued by companies or governments to you as the investor. In return for the investment, the investor will receive a fixed rate of interest. Bonds are relatively safer than equity (shares) but are not risk-free because the bond issuers have to be financially strong enough to continue to pay the interest and the principal when due. Many bonds are issued by governments and are therefore relatively safer and hence attract lower interest rates. If you are sucked in by the high yield of a bond, it could well imply the risk is higher to compensate for the risk you are taking as an investor.

Where investors require regular income to sustain their day-to-day lifestyle, as in the case of people in or nearing retirement, bonds are an essential part of the portfolio. Bonds also play a part in risk mitigation and diversification.

If the interest rate is at a record low, for example in the US, and inflation is at about the same level or higher, bonds are not a good option to generate an acceptable return over the long term.

Which investment type one decides on often depends on their availability and the next best alternative. For example, with a booming US market and bonds paying unattractively low rates in the US; in a rising inflation environment; US investors would seem to have few attractive alternatives but to be in the stock market, especially if it is booming.

Some people might see the stock market as too volatile and risky, and the international market as too remote and complex. But the options for investing are improving fast, with new apps and fintech revolutionizing the space. For example, Robinhood through its easy-to-navigate app, no account minimums, and low trading charges, manages to attract many millions to participate in buying and selling of shares. So, continue to watch and learn.

Just search these investment instruments online and you will find an abundant amount of information about their various forms and how to trade in them. It is highly recommended that you understand at least the basics and then try experimenting with trading in small amounts to have a better feel for them.

Chapter 12
Managing Risks

A fortune can be accumulated over a long period of time, but it can all be lost in one day. To prevent such a catastrophe it is crucial that you manage your financial risks. Just like in sport, it is important not just to go on the offense but also to watch one's defence. A good grasp of the trade-off between risk and reward is critical. Being lucky one year does not mean being lucky over the next 20, 30, or 40 years. On the other hand, being too risk-averse could mean missing out on better returns.

Every penny of your hard-earned money is precious to you, especially if you have a humble beginning and are just starting out. So, you need to be careful that your investments not only have a good chance of making money but also that they retain a high degree of asset preservation.

Risks in investing are unavoidable, but they should be calculated risks. Before taking the plunge, you have made the calculations that should losses occur, they will be losses that you can afford. You want to know the risks in every investment purchase and its impact on your overall portfolio. So, while some investments may end up at a loss, there will be gains from others, so that overall, the portfolio will still yield positive and acceptable returns. The proportionality of risk to the overall portfolio has to be carefully evaluated.

While everything seems to be going smoothly, it is important to make sure that there is a fallback should there be any adverse, unforeseen occurrences that could put you and your family in a bad situation. The loss of jobs and income, of life, of health, accidents or disasters could befall anyone. If these happen over a prolonged period of time, this could really destroy our lives and those of our loved ones. Buying insurance coverage, for yourself and your loved ones to cover the risks for life, accidents, education and medical is necessary, unless there is sufficient alternative coverage (for example the state welfare system). The insurance cost is a necessary evil because the stakes are simply too high.

Measures for mitigating risks in investing

1. Invest in well-run countries.

Look to invest in countries that are well-governed, respect the rule of law, and have laws that protect investor interests. For example, The Securities and Exchange Commission (SEC) is a U.S. government oversight agency responsible for regulating the securities markets and protecting investors, so that a listed company is not run by a bunch of cowboys doing whatever they want for their own self-interest, to the detriment of investors. The SEC is entrusted to ensure good corporate governance. It is important to understand how good corporate governance ensures a certain level of responsible behaviour.

As investors, we can take some comfort in that public companies have to comply with disclosure requirements. The Board of Directors will help to overseas the behaviour of the company. The Board will also have a number of independent directors to enhance its independence. Good management also ensures that there are adequate checks and balances and procedures within the organization. The internal auditors play a key role in this. The external auditors have the statutory duty to make sure the company's risks profile is adequately reflected in its public disclosure. The company disclosures include major developments and its financial performance which is reported quarterly. There are laws that forbid misbehaviour by the company, for example, no insider trading is allowed. The mature and developed economies generally have better rules of law, governance, and investor protection relative to the less developed countries.

Countries that are well run tend to provide improved certainties and better outcomes, including better market and investment outcomes. Take for example the US and the performance of the US indexes in the past. See Chapter 22 - Setting goals and monitoring progress.

What we rely on as good corporate governance in the well-run countries cannot be similarly assumed for the less well-run. The finance department could be colluding in creative accounting; independent directors may not be as independent as suggested; the auditors could be compromised; the company bends to the wishes of the State instead of the investors; news reports and so-called experts express may only offer views to promote their own agendas; the stock market has more of the characteristic of a casino. Avoid these poorly managed countries, no matter the reports nor the promise. Be suspicious. Be very suspicious.

If you only invest in your own country, and if your country is small and not well managed, you will run a higher risk. Look at Venezuela, Zimbabwe, and some countries in Asia, for example. You do not need to rely on relatives working overseas to support living expenses back home; you can invest in good countries and regions overseas to give you the kind of diversification you need.

2. Invest in companies with good management.

It is the directors and senior management team that runs a company from day to day. They can run the company well, or they can run it into the ground. They can make money or lose money, which directly affects the company's stock price. The shareholders own the company. The shareholders elect the board to make sure the management runs the company efficiently. As investors, we want the most competent board that will do a great job in picking the right people to form the best possible management team.

Make sure the companies in which you invest have a proven track record of past performance. For public companies, this information is available in the public realm and in the companies' disclosures and reports. There are charts and key performance indicators for any period in the past. Take note of their performance, not just for recent periods but also for the past few years and decades to assess the consistency of their performance. Pay attention to independent analyst comments and real-time alert messages to make sure the companies do not take a turn for the worst but continue on a positive trajectory.

3. Do not ignore the fundamentals

If companies are fundamentally sound and profitable, their vital statistics will indicate as much. The company accounts, in short, *are* the fundamentals. There are momentum trades from time to time that might take the stock price beyond the fundamentals. There may also be times when investment purchases are made just for short-term gains. Chasing these stocks could end badly if you buy at the high end.

To keep a good measure of restraint, always look at the fundamentals of a company; for example, its valuation (example PE ratio), growth rates, a strong balance sheet, a strong profit and loss statement, a very positive cashflow, a wide moat that ensures sustained unrivaled advantage, and good guidance. Not understanding the fundamentals, especially during a period of high volatility, could cause panic and unnecessary risk-taking.

The fundamentals of a company can easily be found online through their company reports. Companies provide regular updates, at least quarterly, of their latest performance and issue guidance for the coming quarters and future outlook. Potential investors should monitor these regular updates and take any necessary actions.

4. Set up alert messages

The market can change fast and drastically, especially in today's connected world where information spreads fast and wide. So, having the latest, trusted information at your fingertips is very important. When the market dips in a big way, the window of opportunity is often short and small. Delayed information is not good information for investors. Most trading platforms have a function for you to set up alert messages to be sent to your phone or email, based on the parameters you set. For example, price changes of a particular stock that has changed more than a certain percent from its averages. Set up instant news, price change, rating change alert messages. This way you will be alerted in the first instant of any sudden drastic change and can take corrective actions to cut losses.

5. Practice dollar-cost averaging

The markets can be very volatile, especially during periods of uncertainty. Equity prices go up and down, sometimes in extreme ways, and sometimes within a very short period of time. The professionals do their best to read into the future movements of the market. Some see the better times ahead while at the same time others see ominous times ahead. For example, some see a lot of cash sitting at the sideline waiting to invest, potentially boosting stock prices, while others see inflation due to too much money being printed and therefore creating a headwind for businesses. So we should not think that we can predict well, and try to pin our hopes of making money by timing the market right.

The strategy of dollar-cost averaging involves spreading out our stock or fund purchases, buying at regular intervals and in roughly equal amounts. Between getting lucky some months and buying at the very lowest price for our investment and buying at an acceptable average overall cost, the latter would be a more acceptable outcome. We cannot afford to lose, but we can afford to make less, so long as it gets us to our end goal. See more discussion in Chapter 15 - Dollar-cost averaging.

6. Practice sound portfolio management

A portfolio is a collection of financial investments, including stocks, bonds, commodities, cash, real estate, art, etc.

A sound portfolio is one that not only tries to optimize returns but critically, minimizes risk. This is done by first assessing an investor's tolerance for risk, the investment objectives, the time horizon, etc. Risks are then mitigated by not just spreading the risk in more than one investment product, but among products that have the quality of compensating for the loss in others. For example, in a pandemic that shuts down the whole country, the manufacturing businesses may be severely impacted, while those in the technological and pharmaceutical companies tend to do better. See Chapter 14 - Sound portfolio management.

7. Invest, not trade

Prices do go up and down in the short term. That's the equity market. But over the long run, if the fundamentals are good, a stock will recover its equilibrium, grow into and live up to its valuation, and provide the long-term average return as expected.

Listen and take advantage of the stock picks recommended by veteran professionals and fund managers running multi-billion portfolios. These recommendations, including cautionary notes, are constantly updated and made available through the business news channels and podcasts. CNBC and Bloomberg are two powerhouses that provide such information to the professionals and the average retail investors. It is important that listeners understand the rationale of the recommendations and make sure they are consistent with their own situation.

8. Diversification

Diversification is an investment strategy to mitigate risk so that the financial impact on the total asset is reduced as a result of not concentrating the risks on just one stock, one sector, one industry, one asset class, one country, or even one currency. The concept is simple; for example, some companies have policies that do not allow too many of the important senior executives to travel on the same plane.

The effect of risk management is much enhanced when used with sound portfolio management – See Chapters 13 and 14 on Diversification and Sound portfolio management.

9. Hedging

A **hedge** is a strategy that tries to reduce the risks to an **investment** or asset. In practice, hedging doesn't usually eliminate risk. Rather, it is used to lessen the financial impact of an otherwise devastating event.

We hedge by buying an investment that has the effect of reducing the risk of losses from another investment. A 'put' option to hedge against losses in a stock position could to some extent reduce the loss in the stock by gains in the option, given a certain time frame.

Let's illustrate with an example.

For example, if you buy a stock at $12 per share. Let's say you pay a premium of $1 to guarantee you can exercise the put option to sell the stock at $10 within a one-year time frame.

If in six months the value of the stock you purchased has increased to $15, then needless to say you will not exercise the put option and will have lost the $1 premium paid. However, if the stock price drops to $8, you can sell it for $10 per share. The loss, in this case, is $2 per share, plus the premium paid of $1 for a combined loss of $3. Without the put option, the loss would have been $4 per share.

Not all investments need to be hedged. If we are confident about our stocks' long-term prospects, we could ride out the short-term price corrections which are often part and parcel of the stock market behaviors. Corrections of 5-10% are not uncommon. Remember that hedging costs money, as seen in the example above, so the expense paid for hedging has to be worth its while.

Diversification is a good way to hedge (see Chapter 13 on Diversification).

Gold has traditionally been used to hedge against volatility and the loss of the value of currencies.

Some keep cash as a hedge against the risk of a major drop in equity. But remember cash is not a good hedge against inflation or currency depreciation.

What is a good natural hedge that costs nothing? Avoid the get-rich-quick mentality, the unnecessary risk-taking, the gambling mentality. Avoid greed. Steady-as-she-goes investing is the way to go.

Case Study on Risk Management

You have invested 90% of your saving of $100k in a portfolio spread between the US, Europe, Asia ETF holding hundreds of company stocks, and some bonds. The remainder 10% ($10k) you have reserved to take advantage of any opportunities. Now you want to use the 5% ($5k) of that to go after those with a greater return but with higher volatility and risk; for example, the ETF that invests in disruption, like ARK.

Let's say in an extreme year, you lose 80% of this investment, the loss would be $4k, which is only 4% of the total of $100k. It is a risk you are mentally prepared for, from the outset. But you also know that if the ETF does live up to expectations in identifying new disruptive technological trends, there could be significant upside. Look at the beginning of the mega-tech, for example. If you had bought $5k of Apple stock 33 years ago it would now be worth around $1m; and $5k invested in Amazon at its IPO in 1997 would now be worth around $6m.

We do not have to be right all the time, we just have to be right some of the time to reap an outsized return. This is the era of tech and growth, and we are fortunate to be living in the midst of it. Obviously, it is not easy to identify these opportunities. We could pay the professionals to scour the globe for them. Instead of buying stocks on such risky bets, an ETF might be a good compromise, i.e. ETFs that actively scour the markets for disruptive technology. The ARK ETFs may just be one of the channels for this. We have to go on the offensive, but also watch our backs. The mathematical probability of gains as against losses has to be in our favour. This has to be a well-calculated risk.

At the other end of the spectrum, investing one's saving in an ETF that tracks the S&P 500, which holds 500 of the largest companies in the US, is more diversified. However, it is still invested only in equity in the US. For the decade 1999-2009, the S&P lost -2%. So, if you are unlucky to have started investing in 1999 and cashing it out in 2009, you have experienced the lost decade, a decade with no return! The story would, of course, be much different if it had been a different 10-year period, or if it had been extended to more than 10 years. As diversified as the S&P is, there is always the risk of a stock market collapse, as happened in 1997 and 2008.

Chapter 13
Diversification

One cannot learn about investing without knowing diversification. Investors have frequently been admonished: spread your risks, "do not put all your eggs in one basket". Simply put, if you invest all your savings into just one company stock, for example, and if the company then goes bankrupt, you would lose all your savings. If you had split the investment into two uncorrelated companies, all things being equal, your risk would have been halved. Diversification does not only mitigate risks but also provides opportunities for better returns by investing in investments of various risk-reward profiles.

It is often tempting to go all-in into one that seems the most rewarding at the moment. However, there is practically no risk-free investment, no matter how slight. The higher the return, the higher the risk. The taking of undue risk could mean you may never reach your goal of financial independence; but with risk control, you have a good chance of getting there; and with discipline and a bit of luck, maybe even sooner.

Diversification can be achieved by investing in investment types that have little correlation with one another in their risk profiles. These could be real property, bonds, ETFs, mutual funds, company stocks, etc. It is important to understand the underlying risks in each of these asset types before purchasing. Some do carry overlapping risks between them. For example, investing in the mega-tech stocks and ETFs tracking the Nasdaq or S&P 500 may have overlapping exposure because the mega-tech is likely to be a component of Nasdaq or S&P.

Diversification can also be achieved by investing across different geographical regions, countries, different sectors, etc. So you will end up having a portfolio of investment made up of components of different asset types and across different regions and sectors. See Chapter 14 – Sound portfolio management.

What is the right percentage for anyone to hold? Some may say 5%, or 10%, while others may even go as high as 20%. Let's illustrate it this way:

You have a portfolio value of $100k. You own a company stock that makes up 80% of the portfolio. The stock tanked and you lost 80% of its value. So this stock has lost $64k, and its value is now $16k. How long do you think it will take for the other 20% of the portfolio ($20k) to help recoup this loss ($64k)? If you assume the market return in the US generally is 10% per year, probably a long time, maybe even never.

So then, you may say, let me diversify as much as possible. Spreading it too thin, however, will hardly move the dial for you in your portfolio overall performance, with little reduction in the overall risk.

Let's use an example: If you invest $10k in a holding, there is a chance that you could lose 20% to 50% of its value, which will translate into a loss of $2k-$5k. If this potential loss is disconcerting, it is probably too large for you. Much also depends on whether the price drop is likely to be short-term. If the potential upside is way higher, and more importantly if the company is fundamentally sound then the price might rebound.

If you are comfortable with neither of the above, then an ETF may be the way to go. For example, an ETF that tracks the S&P 500, is already diversified across 500 of the leading publicly traded US companies.

So, the main objective of diversification is to reduce the overall risk of an investor portfolio. It is not practiced by simply investing in more different investments but also how each of these components combines to give the whole portfolio a risk profile and return that is acceptable (See illustrations of how a portfolio can be crafted to achieve this in Chapter 14 - Sound portfolio management).

Chapter 14

Sound Portfolio Management

An investment portfolio is a collection of assets that could include investments like stocks, bonds, mutual funds, and exchange-traded funds (ETFs). Having a diverse portfolio of investments will help you to achieve the desired return by spreading the risk across different classes of assets: see Chapter 13 - Diversification.

Each of the investment types has different characteristics that could be exploited to achieve the overall portfolio objectives. Some safer instruments have a low-risk profile, while others are higher risk but with higher potential returns. So, depending on the investment objectives of the investor, the portfolio is designed to consist of a balance of diverse investment types.

You may wish to invest in different geographies and sectors to achieve your overall objective. Financial planners can help to set up portfolios after consultation with the investors. In return, the investors pay an annual fee. Whether investors decide to engage the service of a financial planner or not, it is important to at least understand the basics of portfolio construction.

Investment types

As discussed previously, the common types of investment are bonds, mutual funds, ETFs, and individual company stocks. Each of these has its risk-reward profile. Bonds provide regular fixed income, are less volatile, and tend to have a lower risk. While individual company stocks have higher risks and tend to be more volatile, they provide the opportunity for greater capital gains. ETFs normally have holdings of fifty to thousands of different entities. They are traded like a stock on the exchanges. Most of these are passively managed and hence charge a lower fee than the mutual funds which are mostly actively managed by professional fund managers: see Chapter 11 -Understand major investment types.

Funds that track the market indexes

Indexes are used as benchmarks to gauge the movement and performance of market segments. The main indexes in the US are S&P (Standard & Poors), Dow, Nasdaq, and Russell. Each of these indexes groups companies together in a particular segment. The S&P for example, is made up of 500 of the largest US public companies; while companies listed on the Nasdaq tend to be high-tech and growth-oriented companies. So, if the companies in an index have performed well and their share price has risen, this will be reflected in the increase of the index.

There are now many investment products that mirror the movements of these indexes, which in turn reflect the performance of a particular market segment. For example, one can buy ETFs with ticker symbol VOO that tracks the S&P and ticker symbol VGT that tracks Nasdaq (The ticker symbols are generally English letters unique to the specific assets or securities listed on a stock exchange and are used to identify a specific product for trading purposes). These funds will buy shares in most of the companies in these indexes. So when the S&P moves up by 5%, the VOO ETF should move more or less in tandem. By buying an ETF that tracks the indexes, the investor is essentially trying to participate in the prosperity of the broader market the index is representing.

Investment in different geographies – by region

Some of the geographical classifications are US, Europe, Asia, Emerging Markets, World, etc. Investors can invest in any of these regions through an ETF. For Europe, one could invest in the Vanguard FTSE Europe Index Fund ETF Shares with ticker symbol VGK, and for Emerging Markets, the Vanguard FTSE Emerging Markets Index Fund ETF Shares VWO. Each of these geographies has its characteristics and should be understood in building the portfolio so that they complement each other to achieve the overall objectives.

Investment in different geographies – by country

Essentially investors want to know the economic background to the countries in which they are investing. Some countries in the world have been mismanaged. As a result, the unemployment rate is high, inflation is out of control, and corruption is rampant. Companies in these countries cannot be expected to do well and the stock market is stuck in a perpetual slump. Investing in these countries runs a very high risk of poor performance. People in these countries often have to go overseas to earn a living to support families back home.

In contrast, where a country is stable, innovative, respects the rule of law (especially laws that protect investor interests), practices good governance, has a vibrant market economy, and engages a competent and professional management and workforce, then the stock market should naturally continue to grow. The US and Europe still ticks most of these boxes. Investing in more prosperous and well-managed countries overseas helps to diversify and alleviate many of the domestic risks.

Investment in different sectors

We want to know what sectors will do well. We also want to know in what business the companies in which we invest are engaged. Some of the major sector classifications are technology, financials, industrials, real estate, healthcare, and commodities. These could be further broken down into sub-sectors for more targeted investment. For example, in the technology sector, the sub-sectors include semiconductors, software, or technology hardware, among others.

To illustrate, some of the global market leaders in their respective sectors with whom we may be familiar are:

Banks/Finance: JP Morgan, Goldman Sachs, Citi, Bank of America

Content: Netflix, Disney

Semi-conductors: Nvidia, AMD, Intel, Qualcomm

Auto: General Motor, Ford, Tesla

Technology: Facebook, Apple, Google, Microsoft, Amazon

Retail: Amazon, Walmart

Pharmaceutical: Johnson & Johnson, Pfizer, Merck, BMY, etc

The market leaders in the various sectors often change, depending on their performance. Each of these occupies its niche in the space which could from time to time fall out of favour. So, listening to updates on the news update is important to protect one's investment. All things being equal, it is of course safer to buy the market leaders. They are leaders for good reasons and therefore command a premium in their prices. However, be sure not to overpay even for the leaders.

Each sector has its characteristics that may carry its profile on risk, growth prospects, dividend payouts, volatility, etc. For example, the commodity markets are usually more volatile as they fluctuate more widely but they may also offer a good dividend payout. Technology offers more growth but may have relatively less dividend payout. So if a young investor's preference is to go for growth and is not relying on the dividend payout for regular income, the technology sector should be given its due weight in the portfolio.

Investing in solid and profitable companies

(See also Chapter 19 - The art and science of stock picking.)

A simple high-level portfolio might just consist of:

60% equity

40% bonds

In an environment where bonds are yielding very low return, the desire to look for yield will push investors towards equity, for example, with the following portfolio:

90% equity

10% bonds

However, the above is too broad-brush. So, investors may break it down further:

20% World equity

30% US equity

20% Europe equity

10% Emerging Markets equity

10% Bonds

10% Cash

Of course, a portfolio could be more elaborate. It could be further subcategorized (with some overlaps), as follows:

Illustration 23 - Example of a portfolio with different components:

Category	Investment	Planned Porfolio %	Planned Porfolio ($)	Rationale
Index	US - S&P	20%	20,000	Diversify broadly into broad US large cap
Index	US - Small cap	15%	15,000	Diversify broadly into broad US small cap
Index	US - IT (Nasdaq)	20%	20,000	Diversify broadly into broad US of mostly technology companies
Stock	US - IT stock	5%	5,000	Company stock for enhanced returns
Sector	US - Heath care stock	5%	5,000	Diversify into healthcare
Sector	US - Financial stock	2%	2,000	Diversify into finance
Sector	US - Other stock	3%	3,000	
Type	Bond	5%	5,000	Diversification into fixed income and offset volatility of equity
Geography	Europe	8%	8,000	Diversify into Europe
Geography	China	5%	5,000	Diversify into China
Geography	Asia (Ex China)	5%	5,000	Diversify into Asia
Geography	Emerging	2%	2,000	Diversify into emerging economies
Geography	World	0%	-	Diversify into global equity
Type	Other		-	
Type	Cash	5%	5,000	For emergency and investing opportunities
Total		100%	100,000	

A well-crafted portfolio could enhance overall investment returns while minimizing risk.

In addition to the investment in the subsidized retirement scheme, one may consider investing through an Asset Manager (for example, Fidelity, UBS). You could also trade directly in the stock market on a brokerage platform such as Charles Schwab, Interactive Brokers, or Fidelity. After several years of investment, the assets may be spread across a few channels. It will be necessary to capture all these holdings under one umbrella so that their relative proportion can be monitored to achieve the overall objectives - see Illustration 24 below - Portfolio details.

Illustration 24 – Portfolio details

Name	Market Value ($)	% of Portfolio	% of Overall Portfolio	Co. stock	ETF	Bond	Cash	US - S&P	US IT Stock	US Stock - other	Bond	Europe	Emerging	Other
				Investment type				Region & Sector						
Own Direct Investment														
Emerging	1,000	29%	5.0%		1,000									
S&P 500	1,000	29%	5.0%		1,000								1,000	
Apple	1,000	29%	5.0%	1,000				1,000						
ARK	500	14%	2.5%		500				1,000					
Total	3,500	100%	0	1,000	2,500	-	-	1,000	1,500	-	-	-	1,000	-
401K														
Bond	1,000	13%	5.0%			1,000					1,000			
Equity	6,500	87%	32.5%		6,500			6,500						
Total	7,500	100%	38%	-	6,500	1,000	-	6,500	-	-	1,000	-	-	-
Health Insurance Investment														
S&P 501	2,000	67%	10.0%		2,000			2,000						
Growth	1,000	33%	5.0%		1,000				1,000					
Total	3,000	100%	15%	-	3,000	-	-	2,000	1,000	-	-	-	-	-
Employee Stock	5,000	100%	25.0%	5,000					5,000					
Cash	1,000	100%	5.0%				1,000							1,000
Total Invested Assets	20,000	100%	100%	6,000	12,000	1,000	1,000	9,500	7,500	-	1,000	-	1,000	1,000
%				30%	60%	5%	5%	47.5%	37.5%	0.0%	5.0%	0.0%	5.0%	5.0%

Proportionality is also important in a portfolio. A risky investment while promising a higher return, cannot occupy too large a proportion of the entire portfolio. Much also depends on the particular investment fundamentals and the risk it carries. There are no clear-cut right or wrong numbers because each investor has their own individual circumstance. It comes down to the amount that the individual investor can afford to lose. For example, someone who is still young and with a lot of reserves may find it tolerable to invest in something with the promise of high reward over a very long time horizon (for example, hedge funds).

Generally though, if investors want to bet on the higher growth and relatively greater risk investment, like the unproven but promising new start-ups, this sector may occupy no more than 5% - 10% of the entire portfolio. Should this not work out, the most that the investor could lose is 5% - 10% of their entire assets. For example, some may allocate no more than 5% of the total asset to cryptocurrency because of the uncertainties and volatility, even though many experts are predicting long-term high returns from this asset class.

Chapter 15
Dollar-cost Averaging

Because the stock market goes up and down all the time, and no-one can time the market consistently, it is better not to be caught buying an outsize amount at the top of the market when the price of the stock is high.

So if you invest at regular intervals over a sufficiently long time, the purchase costs will likely capture the price at both the high and low points of the market, so that the average cost of purchases will hopefully be near the middle, or with luck, towards the bottom end. Mathematically, the longer the time the purchases are spread over, the better it smooths out the extremes.

In a market that is fundamentally strong and consistently growing, stock prices could be at a richly and fully valued level and could last a few years because the markets are generally forward-looking. An investor who goes all-in with one lump sum could well end up buying at the high end of the average cost. If the market then has a series of significant drops, there is no more cash to take advantage of the opportunities. Worse, the market may take years, decades, if at all, to recover its previous high. For an investor, this may be a loss they cannot afford.

Instead of buying at the high, some investors choose to wait for a major correction. That waiting could turn out to be years. While waiting, the cash is, in the meantime, sitting in unproductive assets, or possibly one that may even lose value, due to currency depreciation, inflation, etc. The train may then take off, leaving the investors further and further away, which is possible, because, after all, this is a growing economy.

We want to buy low and sell high. Or if we have to buy high, hope that it will go higher. But since we have no predictive ability, and we want to start investing productively, a good approach would be dollar-cost averaging. We want to get on board at a cost that has a good chance of making money.

Another way to play this is to start nibbling when prices drop by a certain percentage from its 100-200 days average, for no fundamental reason. When it drops further, take another bite, until it eventually reaches the targeted bottom price level (for example 20% drop from its 200-day average), with no deterioration in the fundamentals.

The two key features of this dollar-cost averaging approach are 1) to make a regular investment, 2) instead of one lump sum, break it into smaller average sizes. So, if an investor has $10k to invest and has identified a good stock, they could invest $3.3k per month over 3 months, or $1k over 12 months. If during this period, there is a major correction for no fundamental reason, making the valuation compelling, the buy-in could be expedited.

Let's illustrate with an example – see Illustration 25 below.

Actual Unit Purchase Cost ($)	Units	Cost of Purchase ($)	Actual Unit Average Purchase Cost ($)
5	100	500	
10	100	1,000	
15	100	1,500	
	300	3,000	10

If you practice cost averaging, you would have bought the stock consistently over a period of time. In this example, let's say, you bought 100 units at $5, another 100 at $10, and another 100 at $15, giving you an average of $10/unit. Historically the S&P has returned about 10%. So if the average cost of the stocks/ETF purchased is $10, after 10 years, the price should have been $20, i.e.10%*10 years (assumed simple average). So, as planned, you achieved a 10% return per year.

If you had not practiced dollar-cost averaging and bought the shares of 300 units all in one go in the following three scenarios. Scenario 1) cost at $1,500, 2) $3,000, and 3) $4,500 respectively.

See Illustration 26 as follows:

Scenario	Actual Unit Purchase Cost ($)	Units	Cost of Purchase ($)	Selling Price	Return	% Return Over 10 Years	% Return / year
1	5	300	1,500	6,000	4,500	300%	30%
2	10	300	3,000	6,000	3,000	100%	10%
3	15	300	4,500	6,000	1,500	33%	3.3%

If you had gone all-in under Scenario 1, you could achieve 30% growth. If you did not, you could end up in Scenario 3, with only 3.3%. In real life, the scenario with some retail investors could be much worse, sometimes driven by impulse or greed. In a market bubble, the investor could have joined the frenzy and bought the stock at $50, and the bubble burst soon thereafter. This could seriously derail the retirement plan, possibly postponing the retirement by years. It is therefore a much better strategy to try to make a profit as planned than to take unnecessary chances. Remember that one can be lucky sometimes but not all the time. Dollar-averaging improves your odds of winning, although sometimes it may take a bit longer to get the required results.

Chapter 16
Expenses Matter

There are different expenses and costs involved in investing and holding an investment. These expenses could be the strong headwind that hinders an investment from achieving its expected return.

Many investors are not aware of the expenses related to their investments. Some of the expenses are not transparent because they are withheld at source, or not divulged to the investors. The fine print can often be too fine and too technical to understand. Many investors simply do not bother to even try and understand. Many are too trusting of the companies and their consultants. Some consultants even work to their own self-interest and do not voluntarily disclose information on fees etc.

Some investors think that fees don't amount to much. What's the big deal about one or two percentage points, right? You could be seriously wrong. A fraction of a percentage point here and there soon adds up to a significant percentage cut on your return. Like death by a thousand cuts, each taking a slice off your hard-earned investment money. Compounded over time, this could make a world of difference. When excessive, the difference is not just lower returns, it could actually turn a profitable investment into a loss-making one. It sometimes feels like the investors are feeding everyone along the food chain and that everyone makes money except the investors.

Expenses and fees are borne by investors at various stages in the investing process. They can be deducted at source, or they can be charged directly to investors; they may be charged monthly, quarterly, yearly or as a one-off. They can be transactional or based on the asset base. They can also be based on a pre-defined outcome. The point is that unless you take an interest, and you should, you may not know what has hit you; only discovering decades later when you are ready to cash out, that the final result has fallen well short.

With so many of the processes now automated and digitalized, fees have been dropping in recent years. If you are starting, compare and negotiate the fees between different funds. If you have been with the same investment companies and consultants for some time, you need to find out what you have been charged and ask for serious reductions. The asset management companies often enjoy institutional rates (as opposed to retail rates) with the fund-issuing companies. These institutions may choose to pass on part of the discount to their VIP clients. If you are only a small investor, you're unlikely to get many preferential fees.

Let's look at a scenario:

You engage a financial planner. The financial planner then recommends buying a mutual fund. Let's assume the fund is to seek investment opportunities in companies in the S&P. The financial planner charges 1% per year on the AUM (asset under management). This will be charged regardless of gains or losses in the period.

The mutual fund companies will charge a 2-5% sales commission to sell the mutual fund. This is a one-off. So if this is held over five years, it will be 1/5 of the 2-5%. This is sometimes negotiable if the volume is significant enough. For this example, let's assume the investor pays 3%.

The fund managers of the mutual fund will charge a management fee for administering and managing the fund. This could be below or above 1% per year. The fee is deducted by the fund managers before the net return is accrued to the investors.

Assume the S&P this year has gone up by 10%. Let's also assume the fund managers, though active managers, only managed to perform as well as the market. This is not an absurd assumption, because Active Managers have had difficulties consistently beating passive funds like the ETFs.

So the net return of the investment is:

Gross return: 10%

Less: fund manager's fee: 1%

Less: financial planner's fee: 1%

Less: one-time commission (assume held over many years)

Net return before tax: 8%

If one is liable for 20% tax (capital gains/dividend),

The net of tax return becomes 6.4%.

Further, if you assume the inflation rate is 3%

You are only ahead by 3.4% (6.4%-4%).

Bear in mind the one-time commission paid for the mutual fund; if the mutual fund is held for only a year, the commission will set the return back by another 3%. So this is starting to look less and less appealing. At this rate, it is hard to build wealth quickly. For all the risks you bear in investing in equity, this is beginning to look like inadequate compensation.

Let's say, instead of engaging the financial planner, you bought an ETF tracking the S&P online yourself. The only fee paid will be the fund fee charged by the fund manager which is 0.03%. So the net return before taxes is almost 8%. Building wealth looks much better.

That is not to say financial planners do not serve any useful purpose. Far from it, especially in the areas of risk and tax optimization. For those with millions and more, there is too much to lose to go it alone, not to mention the amount of administrative work. For others who could screw things up big time if left to their own designs, leaving the valuable assets to the professionals would be a smart thing to do.

If you are a small retail investor, it is almost inevitable that you need to be financially literate. Engaging a consultant to look after your assets will not do away with that need.

Common fees and expenses

Fund management fee

Fund managers may manage a fund actively or passively. Where it is managed actively, the fee is typically 1% or more. Where this is managed only passively, the fee could be as low as 0.03%. Mutual funds are usually actively managed, whereas ETFs are mostly passively managed. For more explanation on these investment types see Chapter 11 - Understand major investment types.

Advisor fee

Investors that do not have the time, the knowledge, or the confidence to handle the investing themselves, could engage the services of financial advisors to achieve their investment objectives. These professionals could be an Asset Manager, Wealth Manager, Financial Planner, Private Banker, or variants of these. Typically, they help you formulate a portfolio to reach your goals. For this service, they charge 1% or more on the asset under management; less if the amount invested is large, perhaps in the millions.

Sales commission (or 'buy-in fee')

Mutual funds are typically sold to retail investors through a financial intermediary, such as a broker, financial planner, or investment advisor. The retail investors pay a one-off sales commission to the intermediary for effecting any transactions. The fee may be quoted in the official prospectus at 5%, but the intermediary may offer a discount on this rate.

Trading fee

This is the fee for buying or selling shares/ETFs on the trading platform. This is a one-off fee based on the transaction made; so the more you buy and sell, the more fees you will incur. Different platforms charge different rates. Some US platforms offer free trading but in Asia and elsewhere, fees are charged that could become significant for the frequent traders and those trading small amounts at a time.

Custody fee

Banks and brokerages can hold the investments for retail investors after they have been purchased. For this service, they sometimes charge a custody fee. The fee is normally immaterial relative to other expenses but retail investors should still be aware of every cost that could add up very quickly.

Exchange rate conversion

This is a cost incurred for converting money from one currency to another. This conversion is necessary for investors buying stocks in a foreign currency different from their home currency. For example, a Malaysian deciding to purchase US company stock, or ETF domiciled in the US, will have to first convert their Malaysian ringgit (RM) into US dollars (USD). The exchange rate often varies between brokerage platforms and at different times and dates.

Let's use a simple example.

An investor wants to buy $10k of Apple stock at USD125 per share. That would buy 80 shares. The bank quoted the exchange rate of RM4.2 to USD 1. The Malaysian investor will have to come up with RM42k. The brokerage platform they trade on is quoting RM4.5 to USD 1. Their RM42k will buy USD 9333.33, which only buys them 74.66 Apple shares, instead of 80.

Let's say, overnight, Apple's share prices have gone up to USD130 and the exchange rate becomes RM5 to USD 1. Now their RM42k will only buy USD8400. With this, they can now get only 64.6 Apple shares (RM8400/130).

So be wary of the potential currency depreciation, as well as the subtle costs due to the currency exchange rates charged by the banks and the brokerage platforms.

This is a cost that cannot be ignored.

Let's look at another example with greater and more sinister implications:

An investor converted USD10k into RM28k, 25 years ago, at the exchange rate then of USD1 to RM2.8. With RM28k they bought a Malaysian company stock. Assuming the stock price has not changed for the past 25 years, they now decide to take the money back to the US. The shares are sold for RM28k and converted to USD. The exchange rate now has deteriorated to USD1 to RM4.2. They now face a return of $6.67k, a drop of 33.3%.

There are many examples of currencies that at one time or another lost a lot of value. Countries like Venezuela, Indonesia, Zimbabwe, Argentina, etc to name but a few. Investing in countries with a history of huge currency volatility is highly risky. In the example above, imagine that, instead of Malaysia, the investor had invested in Zimbabwe. The loss would have been catastrophic due to the currency's serious depreciation.

It would be ideal if we live in a country with a strong currency that appreciates and is universally accepted. For most, we have no control over the fate of the country and its currency. So our weak and declining local currency means a deterioration of living standards. To invest in countries with a strong currency and strong fundamentals and hence performance, would be a good hedge. Investing in stronger countries would be a relatively good bet, rather than the other way around. However improbable, currency risk is always present and should be understood.

The effect of expenses and taxes

Let's illustrate the significant impact that expenses and taxes could have on your returns in the table below. The actual numbers depend on the countries and their individual tax arrangements but it illustrates the need to scrutinize the overheads in any investment.

Illustration 27 – The impact of expenses and taxes on investment returns.

	Mutual Fund ($)		ETF - VOO ($)	
Investment	Rate	10,000	Rate	10,000
Returns:				
Assume 10% increase in value of the shares		1,000		1,000
Dividend 1.5%		150		150
Reduced by:				
Expenses:				
Asset management/financial planner fee	1%	(100)		0
Fund manager fee	1%	(100)	0.03%	(3)
Trading fee	0%			
Buy-in/sales commission*	2%	(20)		
Custody fee				
Taxes:				
Capital gains	20%	(200)	0%	0
Dividend tax	20%	(30)	15%	(23)
Estate duty	0%	0	0%	0
Net return		700		1,125
% return		7.0%		11.25%

*Buy-in/sales commission - one-off, apportioned over 10 years, assumed holding period
Note: the dividend yield, fee and tax rates are assumed for this illustration

In the example above, the retail investor chooses to DIY and invests $10k in an ETF with low expenses and is fortunate enough to live in a country with no capital gains tax and where dividend tax is only 15% because of the bilateral agreement between the country and the US. Because of the low expenses and the low taxes, the investor essentially pockets every cent of the investment made.

Another retail investor may go another route, engaging a financial planner who happens to think that buying a mutual fund is the way to go. The planner charges a 1% fee for their service. The fund manager of the actively managed mutual fund also charges 1%. In addition, there is also a 2% sales commission charge for buying the mutual fund. Assuming the investor holds the mutual fund for 10 years, the annual average cost of the commission will be 0.2%. If the investor is not so fortunate and lives in a country that taxes 20% on capital gains and another 20% on dividends received, then the result in this scenario is a difference of more than 4% on the annual return. If the investor keeps the investment for 10-30 years, the compounded effect is as follows:

Illustration 28 - Compounding effect of lower expenses and taxes over 10-30 years

Year	Starting Balance ($)	Investment Return (%)	Investment Balance Plus Return ($)	Starting Balance ($)	Investment Return (%)	Investment Balance Plus Return ($)
1	10,000	7.0%	10,700	10,000	11.25%	11,125
2	10,700	7.0%	11,449	11,125	11.25%	12,375
3	11,449	7.0%	12,250	12,375	11.25%	13,767
4	12,250	7.0%	13,108	13,767	11.25%	15,315
5	13,108	7.0%	14,026	15,315	11.25%	17,037
6	14,026	7.0%	15,007	17,037	11.25%	18,953
7	15,007	7.0%	16,058	18,953	11.25%	21,085
8	16,058	7.0%	17,182	21,085	11.25%	23,455
9	17,182	7.0%	18,385	23,455	11.25%	26,093
10	18,385	7.0%	19,672	26,093	11.25%	29,027
11	19,672	7.0%	21,049	29,027	11.25%	32,291
12	21,049	7.0%	22,522	32,291	11.25%	35,922
13	22,522	7.0%	24,098	35,922	11.25%	39,962
14	24,098	7.0%	25,785	39,962	11.25%	44,456
15	25,785	7.0%	27,590	44,456	11.25%	49,455
16	27,590	7.0%	29,522	49,455	11.25%	55,016
17	29,522	7.0%	31,588	55,016	11.25%	61,202
18	31,588	7.0%	33,799	61,202	11.25%	68,085
19	33,799	7.0%	36,165	68,085	11.25%	75,741
20	36,165	7.0%	38,697	75,741	11.25%	84,258
21	38,697	7.0%	41,406	84,258	11.25%	93,733
22	41,406	7.0%	44,304	93,733	11.25%	104,273
23	44,304	7.0%	47,405	104,273	11.25%	115,998
24	47,405	7.0%	50,724	115,998	11.25%	129,042
25	50,724	7.0%	54,274	129,042	11.25%	143,553
26	54,274	7.0%	58,074	143,553	11.25%	159,696
27	58,074	7.0%	62,139	159,696	11.25%	177,653
28	62,139	7.0%	66,488	177,653	11.25%	197,631
29	66,488	7.0%	71,143	197,631	11.25%	219,854
30	71,143	7.0%	76,123	219,854	11.25%	244,577

At the end of year 30, at the return of 11.25%, the asset value is $244,577, as opposed to just $76,123 at 7%.

The difference is stark.

To summarise: to minimize expenses, the following should be considered:

- Buy passively managed funds instead of actively managed ones

- DIY instead of engaging an Asset Manager/Financial Advisor

- Understand the fees, expenses, and costs involved at each level and negotiate, especially if you have been a long term and substantial customer

- Understand the taxes of any transactions and minimize their impact through tax planning

- Choose a lower fee option. For example, use a Robo-advisor instead of a human one; trade online yourself instead of having traders execute the trades

- Try the hybrid option. Instead of having the entire portfolio under the management of the financial planner or asset manager, the investor could have a portion of the portfolio in ETFs that can easily be bought online through a brokerage platform and held long term, leaving the rest of the portfolio to professional management. For example, many retail investors have substantial core holdings in ETFs that track the S&P and Nasdaq for the long term. It may not be necessary to have this under professional management for which one pays an annual fee. This would cut down the annual expense proportionately and could offer significant savings in the long term.

Chapter 17

Tax Matters

Countries need taxes to fund public works and services and to build and maintain the infrastructure used in a country. Some of the most common taxes are:

Personal income tax

Individuals have to pay income tax on their salary and other income. Some countries only tax their tax residents on income derived in the country, while others also tax on their overseas income.

Corporate tax

Companies normally pay corporate tax on their profits in the country in which they operate. For investors, a country that imposes a higher corporate tax rate will mean less after-tax earnings for the investors.

Dividend tax

Dividends are profits that companies have made that they distribute to shareholders, as an incentive to them to continue their support of the company stocks. These are usually issued quarterly, though they could also be made monthly, semi-annually, or annually. Some companies may choose not to distribute dividends but keep the profit for the companies' future development. However, for those who do pay out, a dividend tax will normally be imposed on the funds distributed. This tax is normally withheld by the companies and paid directly to the government, so that the amount is received net of tax by the investors. The higher the tax rate, obviously the less attractive the dividend becomes.

Some countries may impose this tax on their residents and their foreign investors. The tax is deducted/withheld in the country in which it is domiciled, and/or in the country of the investor. Let's illustrate with an example:

A Malaysian investor holds VOO, an ETF domiciled in the US. Assume it now distributes a gross dividend of $100. As the countries have no bilateral agreement with each other, the dividend tax is generally charged at 30%. The dividend tax is withheld at the US side for the US IRS, the net dividend of $70 will go into the account of the investor. Malaysia does not tax dividends received from the US, so the total dividend tax the investor pays is $30.

If the Malaysian investor had chosen to invest in VUSD (the equivalent of VOO), an ETF domiciled in Ireland, which has a bilateral agreement with the US, only 15% dividend tax would be withheld on the US side.

If the investors were US tax residents, the dividend tax rate would have been 20% generally, subject to certain conditions.

Investors have to be aware of what taxes have been withheld and paid at each level. Also, the fact that they have been withheld at source and not paid by the investors does not mean no taxes have been paid.

Capital gains tax

This tax is levied on the capital gains made on investments or assets held. Capital gains are the gains in the investment value over its original cost to the investor e.g. If VOO (a US domiciled ETF) was bought for $20,000 and at the time of sale it has risen to $30,000, the capital gains would be $10,000. If the capital gains tax rate is 20%, the tax will be $2,000, the net gains after tax accrued to the investor would be $8,000.

If you invest in foreign company stocks, it is important to find out what capital gains taxes are imposed in both your country and the foreign country. Using the previous example, if the investor of the VOO ETF were a Malaysian, no capital gains tax will be levied by the US at the time of the sale. Malaysia does not generally impose a tax on capital gains tax. The US person will, on the other hand, suffer capital gains tax, which could be about 20%. So the return on this investment for the Malaysian is 20% higher than his US counterpart, due to the difference in the capital gains tax rates, all things being equal.

Consumption tax

This is another avenue the government uses to increase its tax revenue – through taxes on the consumption of goods and services. This means the more you consume, or purchase as an end-user, the more tax you will pay. This tax is included in the purchase price of the products being bought by the consumers. So, in a country that imposes personal income tax and consumption tax, an ordinary citizen could pay income tax on the monthly salary; then, with the after-tax salary, pay even more tax on any daily necessities they purchase.

Estate tax

Some countries impose estate tax on assets that pass from the deceased to the beneficiaries, subject to some conditions. So, if a person is fortunate enough to have some surplus to pass some down to their loved ones, they could be liable for estate duty on the assets, effectively taking away part of their assets.

You would have thought someone who has done their best for their country, looked after themself, their family and given to the poor, would be given a break at the end of their life. Unfortunately, even at the end, the Government still wants more out of them. In some countries, a person could literally be taxed to death. So, understanding something about tax may help to lighten that burden.

Let's look at an example: Many non-US residents invest in the US stock market, often in company stocks or ETFs. Non-residents investing in US-domiciled instruments, including US company stocks and the US-domiciled ETFs, are liable to US estate duty of up to 40%, with an exempt amount of only $60k. The exception to this is if there is a bilateral agreement between the US and the investor's home country, in which case the tax may be reduced or exempted.

So, the assets inherited by their loved ones can be greatly affected as a result.

How many of us think about death until we are about to pass? Perhaps we think we are too young to die. Unfortunately, no one is too young to die! So should we think about death and taxes when we are just starting to invest? Unfortunately, the answer is 'yes'. There is a whole industry catering to estate planning. Significant investments could incur a significant amount of tax and should be given due forethought.

So we now know that tax is a significant factor, that impacts investment return - see Illustrations 27 and 28. Though this is a complex subject for many untrained investors, there are some basics that every investor must know. Search online for a more detailed explanation of each of the above-mentioned taxes or speak to your tax consultant for efficient tax planning that may save significant tax dollars for you.

Tax laws of a country change regularly to satisfy a country's own needs. They are also very different between countries. This makes the subject of tax, including the implications for the average investors, particularly complex and hard to keep up with.

To educate yourselves on the basics of tax as it impacts investment decisions, do this:

- Identify the major and common tax types (see above).

- Search online for the specific tax issues as they apply to your country and yourself.

Tax evasion is a serious offense in most jurisdictions. No investor should ever try to avoid tax. When the issues become complicated and start to overwhelm, or especially when the amount involved becomes significant, it is time to get advice from the tax legal counsels or the tax accountants. Tax evasion is never worth it.

Chapter 18

The Macro Picture

We cannot invest by just staring at a desktop or a computer screen. It is important to lift your head to see what's going on in the wider world. One cannot effectively invest with a narrow view, limited to only what is in front of us. The macro view of the world – the big picture – is part and parcel of the knowledge required in any investment decision. Before investing we may want to ask:

- Where is the world now and where is it heading? Where will we be in 10-30 years' time?

- Which regions will be trouble spots and which countries will still be strong and well run, their markets performing well?

- What catastrophes/crises, economic, geopolitical, and otherwise, could befall the world, and in which continents and which countries?

- What are the disruptive trends?

- How is my country and the countries around the region performing, economically and otherwise? How will it affect me, now and in the future?

For most of us, we have some idea of where we are in the scheme of things. We walk the streets, read the news and study the views of experts. We then form some basic views of where we are and where we could be heading. One of the most important ways is to read widely. Fortunately, in this digital and connected world, a lot of this information is within touching distance. We can now hear from the most diverse audience, instantly, freely, and at any time. Any information in any location is now available and accessible. We just have to have that desire to want to know and to keep our eyes and ears open.

Let's look at the situation as the covid-19 pandemic emerged and developed in the first half of 2021:

News broke that a certain virus was spreading in a large country and big cities started to go into total lockdown. Other countries responded by barring flights from the country. Soon many countries reported high infection rates and deaths; medical facilities became overwhelmed, even in the advanced countries. The medical experts say they were still trying to understand how the virus spreads and there was conflicting advice as to how to reduce infection. Many countries did not have the therapeutics nor the vaccines to deal with it. Even political leaders at the highest level were infected. Soon more countries were in lockdown, travel between countries was stopped, hundreds of thousands died, many without medical help. Restaurants could not operate, airlines stopped flying, in the mall people were fighting over toilet paper as supplies ran out because factories were also closed down. Many large companies saw their revenue drop to almost zero. All around the world people stayed at home for months to ride it out. Many people got restless, being told to stay indoors for months on end. Meantime, many people had no income. Political leaders worldwide grappled with the twin issues of saving lives and/or saving the economy.

Starting February 2020, the market started to take notice, dropping by a few percentage points. Each week it dropped further; by March, it had dropped about 30% from the pre-pandemic level.

As an investor you had been waiting on the sideline, waiting for a correction to buy the stocks you have been eyeing. These stocks were growing and making tons of money pre-pandemic but the valuation was full or frothy. Now this situation came out from nowhere. The biggest 'black swan' event one has ever seen.

How did you react to the initial news? How did you invest in 2020, especially starting in February and March?

- Did you buy a lot of restaurant and cruise ship and airline stocks because they were so dirt cheap?

- Did you take the opportunity to buy those stocks that you had always wanted to own?

- Were you too panicky and decided to wait until it was too late?

- Analysing the companies' fundamentals at that time did not seem that useful. So, what was the big picture you saw at the time?

- While everyone was heading for the exit, did you think the party was in full swing? Did you try to catch a falling knife?

Maybe this was what you saw:

You sensed that this was serious. But you knew it would not wipe out the human race; it would pass. We would come out the other side. The world before the pandemic was humming along pretty nicely. But how long would it take to recover? Nobody knows. Your estimate was that it could take two years. The experts were working on therapeutics and vaccines were starting to emerge. You knew some companies may never recover, but you also knew that some big companies had been doing well and would continue to do well through the crisis. You didn't know how to time the lowest point of the market. You didn't know when or if there would be a second greater dip as some experts predicted. You had been eyeing some very large caps with very good growth pre-pandemic and with deep pockets. Signs started to emerge that these companies were relied upon even more during the pandemic. You reasoned that if it dipped to 30% below the pre-pandemic level and could take up to two years to recover, the return would still roughly equate to 15% per annual return.

Now with each big drop, you started to nibble, and with each more significant drop from the pre-pandemic level, the nibble became bigger. For example, the ETF tracking S&P and Nasdaq, the FAANG, or even the ARK ETFs and other stocks (some lost more than half their pre-pandemic price) had dropped their price for no apparent reason other than the pandemic.

By the time it reached the bottom, you had successfully secured some of the stocks you have always wanted to own, at fantastic prices, though not all at the lowest prices.

Some were predicting a bigger second dip. That never came, so you missed out totally on a few bargains. But you were not greedy. You took advantage of the first dip. You did leave some dry powder just in case a bigger second one came around. Even though it did not come, you felt okay because you got substantially what you wanted. You had been waiting for a correction. When it finally arrived, you saw it as it was, a pandemic but also an opportunity. You saw the big picture.

Some of the big picture scenarios include the economic aspects:

The economy

If a country is producing more goods and services each year, then the Gross Domestic Product (GDP) of the country is growing and the country should be doing well. The population will have high employment; prices of daily necessities will be under control; the people will have more on which to spend. General well-being is an unmistakable sign that the economy is doing well. Companies will ride the waves of growth, which of course bode well for investors.

The converse will also be true; investing in poorly run countries where the economy experiences prolonged stagnation; where people are unhappy and struggling economically; is not a good investment.

The stock market

The stock market is a public market for trading stocks and other financial securities like exchange-traded funds (ETFs), corporate bonds, and derivative products. When the economy is not doing well, obviously the stock market will be adversely affected.

Interest rates

Interest rates affect more aspects of our lives than we realize. Let's look at a few scenarios you may have encountered.

If the interest rate is high, fewer people will buy property and real estate prices may drop as a result; the banks will make more money from higher interest income, and therefore create a tailwind for bank stocks; borrowing costs for companies will be higher, leaving less profit for the investors, discouraging capital expenditure and investment, which have to justify the higher loan interest.

In a low-interest rate environment, investors are less likely to want to keep their cash in fixed income/bonds and prefer to look for more return in equity, creating a positive impact on the overall stock market.

Central banks use interest rates as a policy tool to twig the direction of the economy. When an economy is running too hot, central banks may slow it down by raising the interest rate. When inflation is increasing, interest rates tend to increase as well. Higher inflation tends to lead to higher interest rates.

A country borrowing money to finance its many social programs will have to spend more to service the debts, leaving less money for the welfare and development of the country.

A country with persistently high interest rates relative to other mature and advanced countries, therefore, is not a good sign for investors. So investors watch out for the movements in interest rates and interpret their impact on the market.

Inflation

The price of goods and services generally go up over time. The inflation rate measures the price movement of a basket of goods we typically consume. If unchecked, it could wreak havoc on the economy - things become less affordable, the country's currency depreciates, people generally become poorer. Inflation is the silent killer that keeps taking away from us without you even noticing it.

In some countries, e.g. Venezuela, the inflation rate has been astronomical and prolonged. So the money that you earn has to keep up. You might think the safest way to preserve your wealth is to hold tight to your cash. After all, if you tucked away a $100 note under the mattress, after 10 years you will still pull out the same $100 denominated note. But this $100 will buy much less goods in 10 years.

Hoarding your cash under the mattress is disastrous as an investment option. For example, if the inflation rate is 3% per year, putting your savings in a fixed-term deposit earning only 1% per year will mean that your money is shrinking by 2% every year. You are not wealthier but poorer every year. Imagine what will happen if the inflation rate was 10% or more, as in some countries, especially if it strikes just as you are about to retire?

In an inflationary environment, companies tend to make less money unless they can pass on their cost. Inflation that is uncontrolled means that the economy is in a bad shape and the prospects for the stock market is generally not good.

What causes inflation? When supply cannot meet the demand, prices tend to increase. As a result, we see prices rising in commodities, labour costs, daily necessities, and properties, among others.

The Federal Reserve seeks to control inflation by influencing interest rates. When inflation is too high, the Federal Reserve/Central Banks typically raises interest rates to slow the economy and bring inflation down. This could impact business. So investors need to watch closely what they do.

What kind of investment would be a good hedge against inflation? You may want to consider what are called Alternative Assets. These includes things such as gold; digital currencies such as Bitcoin; real estate; and art works. Be sure to read up on each of these asset classes to understand their pros and cons in hedging against inflation.

Exchange rate

As discussed previously, the exchange rate affects your purchasing power and your investment returns. The effect will be more striking if the purchase is made with a weak currency for goods sold in a strong currency.

So importing an airplane from the US by paying for it over time with an ever-weakening local currency will translate to a higher airfare for the local passengers. Similarly, paying for foreign technology, for example, medical products, with a weak local currency will cause increase hardship to the sick as the price of their medicines will gradually increase.

Take Malaysia as an example. The Ringgit to USD exchange rate 10 years ago was 3:1, in 2021 it is 4:1, a depreciation of 32%! So for parents who have saved up RM100k for their children to attend a US university, this can have dire consequences. If they had budgeted for a school fee of USD 32.25k, 10 years later, this could only pay for a school fee of $24.4k. Let's say the parents in their foresight had invested RM100k in a US asset valued 10 years ago at USD 32.25k, at the then exchange rate of RM 3.1: to USD1. Then 10 years later, even without any capital gains, the asset will still be worth USD 32.25k, in Ringgit terms, that is now RM 132.2k.

Imagine the potential uncertainties and downside currency risks over a long investment period. Some of the countries with volatile currency and depreciation risks are Argentina, Venezuela, Iran, Indonesia, Zimbabwe, etc.

Therefore, if you are from one of these smaller countries in the less developed world, diversifying investments in bigger and stronger countries could be a lifeline if your country runs the risk of being mismanaged.

If you live long enough; read, see and hear enough; you should have a view of where the world around you is going. Hopefully, this view is corroborated by the professionals. We can then make an educated guess based on this view. There is no shortcut. Our financial education comes from reading widely, keeping up with the news, living long enough to see the ups and downs, experiencing all sorts of human triumph and tragedies but also experiencing the vicissitude of the market.

You should entertain, nay, welcome opinions. You should be even more responsive to contrarian views, perhaps even more so to those that are critical of your opinions. You understand universal values and the important lessons, especially in ensuring long-term success. You want to be curious about new knowledge, new trends, and at least have knowledge of some of the basics so that you don't look like you are behind the times. The world continues to move forward and constantly transforms. You must take the time to understand the big picture.

These are the complex subjects that economists advise on. But as retail investors, we want to know the basics and their implications on our investments. Keep up to date with the latest knowledge and market information. There is a lot of useful and easy-to-understand information coming at you online and through the cable business news. Let the news run the whole day if you are at home while multi-tasking. It is probably the best financial investment you will make. If you have less time and are always on the go, some podcasts give very timely authoritative recommendations. Instead of paying 1% to try to get it from your consultants, who may not have too much time for the little retail investors, these are almost free! And you do it at your own pace, read whatever suits you! Times have changed; this is now so democratized that everyone who wants to be, can be well informed.

Some of the best sources include Investopedia, CNBC News, Bloomberg. I listen to CNBC to get my stock pick leads. If you think this is too much homework, try it out for only a week, a month, or three months. You may be surprised how much you have missed and how much you learn.

Naturally, there are many occasions when situations arise that will rattle even the most seasoned professionals. Boom-bust cycles can happen every few years or decades; crises happen out of the blue; and the so-called 'black swan' events appear with surprising regularity. When you are confronted with a real-life situation, believe me, there will be panic and fear. These crises affect your hard-earned, precious assets. You are torn between protecting your assets and trying to seize the opportunities they present. Having the broad picture not only helps you to avoid pitfalls, it also helps you to take advantage of it to make some good money.

Investors should have a macro picture of where they see the world, region, or country and where these are heading. Below are some examples, for illustrative purposes:

The macro picture of the sectors

- The world is undergoing a technological revolution

- Artificial intelligence creations become smarter than humans

- New platforms are launching pads for new experiences

- Connectivity makes applications and products quickly become global

- Miniaturization makes the impossible just a few years ago possible

- Big data opens up more insight into complex problems much quicker

- Almost all fronts are open for disruption, creating new demands that never existed before

- Digitalization enables new business models that make old models obsolete overnight

- The world shrinks to within our palms and fingertips, all enjoying and sharing the same thing almost simultaneously.

As a result, growth for the tech sector in recent years has outstripped other sectors. We are seeing the largest of the traditional companies now become relatively small, for example, the oil and gas companies now make up only 2-3% of the S&P, down from 15% in 2008;. The mega-companies with a market cap in trillions are now taking over and continue to grow at breakneck speed (Amazon, Apple, Microsoft, etc) - annual growth at 30-50% is now not unusual. New online experiences create new demands and new markets, boosting revenue exponentially. Unknown start-ups have become global household names in record time. By seeing the big picture, investors have a view of the trends, sectors and themes in which they would like to invest.

While tech has made huge advances in recent years, diseases still kill millions every year; many things still run and are managed manually; the world still has many unsolved problems; many essential items still cost too much. So when we think about robotics, biotech, artificial intelligence, cloud computing, fintech, the internet of things, autonomous products – many are still at the conceptual phase. The full potential of 5G and its enabling properties has yet to be fully felt but without doubt, it will be immeasurable. The world can but move on to 6G and 7G, 8G and beyond. The possibilities are unimaginable, the rewards almost certain.

Imagine what the world will be like if we finally see autonomous vehicles on the roads. We have already seen a proliferation of robots in buildings. But wouldn't it be out of this world to see vehicles darting around on open roads and streets like robots? We are not talking about just more convenience in getting from point A to B. This could change your lifestyle from past generations. There will be less parking, fewer drivers, fewer vehicles, less car fumes, fewer accidents, fewer road rage incidents, no driving under influence. There will also be more time, more fun, more mobility, and more blue sky for everyone. Our cars could become our chauffeur, our mobile home, our holiday home, our office. When it is fully equipped, connected, and powered (battery, solar or other), it will let you play, work, live anywhere.

We crave mobility. That's why the mobile phone has become indispensable. It shrinks the world to within our grasp. Autonomous cars are also mobile and much bigger, better things can be stuffed into them. Our home is our castle. In time to come, our castle could move anywhere in the world. It is not a pipe dream. It could happen before we even realize it. Some are predicting it could happen on a commercial scale in a decade while others suggest sooner. It has been reported Apple is launching fully autonomous cars by 2025. Isn't that like, 'just around the corner'? If you are in your twenties, so what if it does not happen in five years but instead in fifteen? It is starting to happen, you can already smell it!

We are fortunate to be at the cusp of this big change. Could this be a generational investment opportunity? Could we see companies that are at the epicentre of this revolution gain multiple times on their current valuation? The sub-sector within technology could be the autonomous and robotic theme. Players in this technology could include the car and truck companies (example Apple, Tesla), the ride-sharing companies, the logistics and courier companies.

Tech has been the sector that survives any weather, anywhere. Many of the stocks in this sector are not just lucrative but safer, due to their sustained growth and financial strength. Even those sectors outside the technology sector will have to endorse and adopt technology in their operations to stay ahead of the competition. Investment in the technology sector would seem like a good bet for the next 5-10 years. Until the world finds another new thing to get excited over.

The macro picture of the world/region/ country

As I look around the world, there has been no better place to invest in the last decade than in the US. This is not surprising. It is not only the world's superpower but also the world's largest economy. Its spirit of capitalism, corporate governance, innovation, capable workforce, and its values are a recipe for unrivalled competitiveness and consistent performance. The returns achieved in past decades relative to other regions attest to that dominance. Other regions and countries almost pale in comparison. The largest and the most innovative companies are located there. Why invest anywhere else if you have not invested first in the USA?

However, this is not to say there are no issues with the world or the US. The world could be destabilized by a clash of civilizations, differences in ideologies, environmental degradation, geopolitics, etc. The capitalist spirit of the US could be doused by the spirit of entitlement or diluted by demographic and political changes. As we watch from the sideline, it is becoming increasingly divided, so divided that you wonder if at some point in the future it will break apart.

So I try to look elsewhere to see if I could find an alternative. For a country somewhat familiar, I can see that the UK has potential. Post-Brexit, it is free to chart its own course. This is a country that knows how to play hard and work smart. It practices universal values, the rule of law, and has good governance. It may be a much smaller country and smaller economy than the US but the English-speaking world is a large one and includes the Commonwealth of Nations. The former British commonwealth countries include some of the largest economies in Asia and Africa. They are emotionally connected to the UK through history, language, and cultural affinity. It is still the place that most of the English world and those in Europe would want to visit for business, careers, and learning.

The advantage of English-speaking countries should not be underestimated. The most advanced research knowledge is published in English. International business is conducted mostly in English. Innovation requires as big a talent pool as it can access. It can find it in the universe of the English-speaking world. Many countries also still practice the essence of common laws, so doing business together has a common legal ground.

English also connects Europe. European professionals with international career ambitions want to hone their English skills with a career spent in the UK. Europe, a regional economic powerhouse, is just across the channel. The UK's role in the world will be enhanced should the US prove to be less attractive or welcoming; or if the US starts to go down the wrong path, or even implode.

That the UK is an international finance hub is no coincidence. It was borne out of centuries of overseas trade. The international success of the soccer Premier League is also an example of the respect it still commands. In a nutshell, it is a place of decency, the motherland of the English-speaking world, it has a special relationship with the US, and it has a big backyard in Europe. This is the home of Charles Dickens and Shakespeare, the birthplace of many of today's most popular sports, and The Beatles! With this big picture, I started investing in ETF investing in the UK. Now, let's see what they can do.

I watch the world, and especially the US and the UK. Personally, these are my big picture economies (for illustrative purposes) before I even decide in what to invest. You may see things differently but by now I hope you understand my view of the world and how it affects my investment decisions.

Chapter 19
The Art and Science of Stock Picking

A good way to participate in the prosperity of a country is to invest in its equity market. By buying shares in a successful company, you are effectively owning a piece or a share of the company. And successful companies reward their investors with their increasing share prices over the long run. This discussion is especially relevant for the average investor. You do not have to be a professional with the latest, in-depth knowledge to participate.

As discussed previously, the safest way to invest in equity (stocks) is through ETFs and mutual funds. Each of these holds tens, hundreds, or thousands of stocks. The more moderate risk brings moderate returns, as the returns are averaged out across all the holdings.

There are times, however, when stock picking may become appealing. Perhaps you feel strongly that a particular company is going to perform well in the future. This could also improve your overall returns and add a little fun and excitement to your investing strategy.

Buying stocks is relatively risky and stock picking is not for everyone. After all, stock prices depend on the company's performance which could change from quarter to quarter. If you haven't a clue and don't wish to do the research, then this is unlikely to be suitable for you. Do not buy stock with money that you cannot afford to lose.

The stock market is not a casino. You do not make money by blowing on the dice, giving it a roll, then hoping and praying that luck is with you. A company can do well one quarter or one year and badly the next due to management changes, competition, market conditions, political risks, or occasionally some unforeseen circumstance such as covid. Many factors chase the stock prices higher and higher to form a bubble, which could result in significant irrecoverable losses. Unless you are experienced, informed, and have a disciplined approach, the risk is significant.

Perhaps you will end up buying 20 different stocks. The overall return from these 20 stocks may not outperform the S&P, because although some will have gains, some will probably also suffer losses. After all the trouble and hard work of picking stocks yourself, you may still end up not beating the S&P. You are not alone, many professionals face the same embarrassing outcome.

The secret of stock picking is obviously to find something great and hold on to it. Buy good and strong companies that you love and are proud to own for a long time. Don't just buy stocks that you think will offer quick gains. Invest, not trade because very few people are good at timing the market. Rotating in and out of certain sectors is not for everyone, least of all for those with little experience or little time for research.

So how do you find these great companies?

Selecting stocks

In our daily lives, we come across many good products and services widely used by all. For example, we have our personal accounts with the largest and the strongest banks; we use phones that provide the best apps and give us the least hardware problems; we search online for whatever we need each day; we use our desktop to perform our work; we wake up every day and the first thing we check is what our friends say on the social media; we shop for all our daily necessities on our favourite online store; we trust the medication produced by the big pharmaceutical companies; and we sit down to stream movies at the end of a long day. So, we are to some extent familiar with them.

We buy from the best companies; we trust the best companies. They are good at the business they are running, i.e. they are leaders in their particular sectors. These leading companies are always in the news, so we know much about their every move. Examples of some of the leading brands that are trusted around the world include:

Content – Netflix, Disney

Online store – Amazon

Phone – Apple

Social media – Facebook

Desktop and software - Microsoft

Bank – JP Morgan, Citi

Search engine – Google

What makes them great and promising companies? They may stand out in your mind for a number of reasons:

Disney – Many of us grew up watching their movies, and still watch them with our children, repeatedly. We may grow out of their movies (or we may not!) but we will always want our children to live with fantasy and wonder. They are assets that are unlikely to go out of fashion. Actors die and fade away but not Mickey Mouse.

Facebook (Meta) – Recently re-branded as Meta, it is the largest social platform in the world, with 2.8 billion monthly active users in 2021. With so many captive customers, all connected, no wonder its advertising revenue is tremendous. The possibilities of more applications to exploit the worldwide audience are also limitless – take, for example, recent opportunities in merchandising and digital currency.

Apple – The largest company in the world, with $2.1 trillion capitalization. The company has one of the world's largest customer bases hooked on its ubiquitous phones, bundled with a sticky ecosystem. Apple has strong and promising multi-income streams with more in the pipeline, as well as expanded technologies to draw users into its ecosystem e.g. electric cars, wearable technology, and healthcare.

Google – A search engine so dominant that it is almost a monopoly. It has become so well-known that the brand has become generic. It brings the world to our fingertips. Thanks to Google we are always in the know about the world around us. No wonder its advertising revenue has been phenomenal, complemented with other significant income streams, with more to come from developing new technologies.

So when the professionals come on air to discuss and recommend these familiar well-known names and the reasons for buying their stock, we want to check them out. Let's check out a few of these mega-tech companies below to see if they might suit your portfolio:

Illustration 29 - Big Tech past performance

Compound Annual Growth Rates					
No. of years	Microsoft	Amazon	Apple	Facebook	Google
1	37%	30%	56%	43%	65%
2	43%	36%	70%	36%	46%
3	37%	26%	40%	19%	28%
5	37%	35%	39%	23%	26%
Market Cap	1.9T	1.6T	2.1T	932b	816b

Note: The data above was extracted during the time of the writing and could have since changed. The table is for reference and illustrative purposes only. Any purchasing of the products should refer to the latest official documents.

These companies are big, strong, and profitable! Together, they make up more than 20% of the S&P which contains 500 of the largest public companies in the USA. If the S&P on average returns 10% in the past decade, these behemoths return much more and are getting even bigger, stronger, and more profitable! Still, you should browse their financial statements to confirm how 'great' they are in the current market. As investors, we do not want to overpay, even for 'great' things.

Knowing that these mega stocks have achieved such stellar performance over the past few years and the consensus that the trend will continue, what is a better strategy: hold them long-term, or try to rotate them in and out between sectors as they are perceived to be in, or out, of favour? Could you really time the rotation well? For an untrained retail investor, a mistimed trade could mean that you lose out at both ends i.e. by rotating out of a sector you could end up selling at the low end, and buying into the new sector at the high end; then at a later stage, come back to the desired long-term hold when it has gone up significantly. Trying to be cute instead of 'steady-as-she-goes' may end up being very counter-productive. How much more do you realistically think you could make switching in and out, especially as an individual investor? Is the consistently stellar performance of some of these mega-stocks that outperformed the S&P by a significant margin still not good enough? Why bother taking on more risk?

Picking the right stocks is just the first part, the second part involves monitoring their performance. Individual stock tends to be more volatile and riskier relative to an ETF which holds hundreds of different company stocks. If you are not prepared to continue to monitor them after the purchase, perhaps ETFs/mutual funds may be a better option for you.

Investing is not about picking the right stocks but the process of picking the right stocks. So be careful if your best-buy ideas came from a casual chat with relatives, friends, or neighbours. Regardless of the source of the recommendations, one must go through a thoughtful and calculated process. For example:

Factors to consider before buying stocks

- Do I already hold too much of it?

- Are they recommended by the professionals in the news debates? What are their arguments for and against?

- Do the financial statements confirm the recommendations (browse the financial statements)?

- What is the consensus valuation – current and forward PE?

- What is the current price, recent peak? Is it based on recent moving averages?

- Is it profitable?

- What are future growth rates predicted to be?

- Is there an overwhelming recommended buy/outperformance by major independent rating agencies?

- How much should I buy, at what price?

So you see, it is less about *which* stocks to pick but more about *why* to pick them.

If the answers to the above are mostly positive, then explore further.

As retail investors, we may not have all the in-depth technical and financial knowledge available to institutional investors. We are unlikely to have the time, nor the resources to obtain them. But we do have the following: we can take advantage of the insights of these savvy investors after they have done their research. We stand on the shoulders of these giants or piggyback on them. Many of these professionals regularly share their advice online and on cable business news.

The open discussions and debates between the professionals can often be conflicting, showing that stock recommendations are often subjective; viewpoints can be either a glass half-full or a glass half-empty. The good thing is that readers can hear both views and make up their minds. Where this is ambivalent, the listener should buy less of the investment or buy something else that seems more convincing. Being a good listener is absolutely essential in obtaining insights and also filtering out the noise that could mislead investors. However, we still have to be smart about whether any of these insights are good for our situation. So, we should follow these few steps:

- Be informed and keep abreast of the macro picture

- Listen to recommendations and the 'for-and-against' arguments

- Be disciplined and follow a thoughtful process

- Check the fundamentals

- Review and confirm the recommendations with the latest analysts' buy ratings.

Also, refer to The Process in Chapter 20 – Be very disciplined in your approach.

Much of the information required for investment decisions are available online and often made available at little or no cost. Retail investors do sometimes have to satisfy certain conditions imposed by the brokerage platforms which provide this valuable information. These sites don't just offer education materials but also the latest research and market information. Retail investors have to filter this information, taking full advantage of the work offered by the professionals.

Some of the most valuable reference information for stock-picking decisions are the analysts' predictions of future earnings; target price of the shares; recommendations to buy, hold or sell; and the reasons for their recommendations, among many others.

We can usually rely on the information for decision-making if we can trust the source. Most professionals in the media are themselves accomplished investors, with multi-billion dollars assets under management. They are putting their firms and their reputation at stake by making recommendations. The news channel also has an ethical duty to make sure the recommendations are not self-interested. For the listeners, the household names recommended as buys are likely to be widely covered by the analyst community. This means they will come up for discussion regularly when there is breaking news. Any recommendations that are too contrarian will usually be challenged on the spot by their peers and will not reflect well on them.

To illustrate: a retail investor does not own any Apple shares. The investment forum on TV has been discussing and debating Apple. This is a mega-stock, the largest by market capitalization, held by almost every institutional investor. Some of the panellists strongly recommend it as a "compelling buy" at $125 and predict 15-20% upside in six months; it is 10% from its peak and below the 200-day average; the PE is not excessive at 28, and the forward earnings will make the valuation even better.

Apple clearly has a few potential major upsides, for example, the product super-cycle; its multi-income stream; products like the wearables; the app services income; the introduction of 5G; healthcare products; the autonomous car; a ton of announced share buybacks; its last quarter earnings report was a blowout; the guidance for the next quarter and to the end of the year is for growth to continue; the annualized return the past five years was more than 30% and the trend remains intact. Any investor should be interested!

So, on hearing all of this upside, the investor wants to confirm their conviction with the fundamentals. It does not take much time to browse the fundamentals. Platforms are now very user-friendly and convenient to browse. For example, see Illustration 30 below to see the key financials of Apple in a glance:

Illustration 30 – Apple key financials

Description	Apple	Explanation
Market capitalization	2.1T	The total dollar market value of a company, by multiplying its stock's current market price by the total number of shares that can be bought and sold by the public.
Current price	$123	The most recent selling price of a stock
Dividend yield:	0.70%	Dividend paid out by a company expressed as a percentage of its share price. The formula is: divide the annual dividends paid per share by the price per share.
PE	28	Price-to-earnings ratio - measures the company's share price relative to its earnings per share
PE forward	24	Price-to-earnings ratio - measures the company's share price relative to its future estimated earnings per share
EPS		Earnings per share, calculated as a company's profit divided by the number of outstanding shares
Q1 2021	1.68	
Q2 2021	1.4	
Q3 2021 (est.)	1	
Q42021 (est.)	1.12	
2021 FY	5.2	
2022	5.2	
200-day moving average	$124	The average closing price of a stock over the last 200 days
Recent peak price (18/1/2021)	$145	
Rating by agencies:		Ratings assigned by analysts or rating agencies
CFRA	4 stars	The best is 5 stars
Argus	Buy	Ranges from buy, hold, to sell
Credit Suisse	Neutral	The stock is expected to perform in line with the expected returns of the market
Reuters	Outperform	Underperform - projected to do slightly worse than the market average, overperform - projected to provide returns higher than the market average
Target prices	$150-160	Analysts' projection of a stock's future price
Revenue growth		The increase, or decrease, in a company's sales between two periods
2021 (estimate)	24.9%	
2020	5.5%	
2019	-2.3%	
Earning growth		The increase, or decrease, in a company's earnings between two periods
2021 (estimate)	39.4%	
2020	3.9%	
2019	-7.8%	

Note: The data above was extracted during the time of the writing and could have since changed. The table is for reference and illustrative purposes only. Any purchasing of the products should refer to the latest official documents.

On the platform, let's say it confirms again that most rating agencies are recommending 'outperform/strong-buy'; their earnings estimates are largely in line as quoted by the panellists; the majority of the target prices are at least 10-20% more from the current level and continue rise, etc. It seems that the stock ticks all the right boxes. Buying at $125 would appear to have more potential for upside than downside. It is a good level at which to be buying the stock.

From the time the retail investor hears about the recommendation, checks it out on the platform and executes the trade, it may take less than half an hour. The process is not too laborious and will become easier after some practice. It is transparent and the retail investor is in full control.

Being disciplined in stock picking is important. If you tend to be impulsive and emotional, even overcome by greed, you run risks that could undo you. If the investor still has reservations despite the positive arguments – maybe because Apple's China sales are a problem, or its app service fees are being challenged by the app developers, etc – then they could set a limit on the price at which to buy; or buy a smaller amount, then buy more when the price drops further.

Sure, the price will sometimes dip after the purchase. That could well happen. However, since the fundamentals have not changed, it should grow into the PE in a few quarters, as anticipated. So, patience is called for.

As with most investments, it will be a good bet if the stock price has the potential for more upside than downside. For example, a growth stock that has grown on average 30% over the past five years, has, for some reason, been drifting sideways for the past six months. Its earnings growth has been phenomenal the past few years and quarters and has again confirmed this growth in the latest quarter. This growth is widely forecast to continue the trajectory. This means the PE is continuing to decline, which makes the valuation that much more attractive. The stock price is now 20% from its recent peak. With no known major negative factors on the horizon, it should be easy to see there is a greater chance that its price is more likely to go up than down within the next few quarters. Maybe it will go down further, say by another 10%, but the odds of it going up by more than that is greater. This is a pretty good bet, don't you think?

Let's take the IT (information technology) sector for example. We know this is a high-risk, high-reward investment for those into disruptive technologies. Many tech companies have enjoyed exponential growth. We do not have the industry knowledge and seem to be always late to the party, missing the boat to reap those high returns. Those professional managers who have in-depth knowledge of the key technologies will scour the global markets to identify opportunities for us. In return, we may have to pay a higher fee for their active management, as opposed to passively tracking the indexes.

We know these companies are potentially more volatile and could be unprofitable for a while, even burning through tons of cash as they develop. Indeed, some may fail. Some will have sky-high valuations. Buying direct is too risky for individual retail investors. So, we could buy ETFs which hold many of these different stocks to diversify the risks of the growing companies.

We know we are investing with a long time horizon in mind, so we can tolerate short-term volatility. Long-term we know it is likely there will be enough successful companies in the ETF holdings to produce the expected overall returns. We just have to make sure the professional managers stick to their fund mandate and constantly update investors on what they do with our money every step of the way.

With this in mind, we searched and indeed found just such a channel, the actively managed ARK funds. ARK Investment Management LLC is an American investment management firm based in Florida that manages several exchange-traded funds (ETFs) that focus on the tech markets. True to form, it sometimes performs exceptionally well, but it has also been volatile. When interest rates started to move up and looked like heading higher, the fund took a dip because to the investors, funding these so-called risky investments just became too expensive and risky. Expert commentators start to question the high PE, the volatility, and the risks.

Some investors panicked. We shouldn't. We have to go back and ask why we bought into these funds in the first place. Didn't we expect these sorts of disruptions? We did not pick the stocks, we picked the tool to do the job. Unless the fund managers have deviated from their mandate or have been poor in the execution of that mandate, this is still the tool to stick with.

When stockholding has exceeded your planned ratio to the overall portfolio, or when the risk becomes unacceptably high (often because its valuation has increased significantly), it is OK to take some of the profits and bring your investments back to the planned ratio.

A stock purchase that may have been good to start with could turn bad for various reasons. Set up email alerts that will alert you to any significant price or other changes. For example, a drop of 20% will trigger a decision to sell and cut the losses.

There has never been a better time to invest. You do not have to be able to afford financial advisors to start investing. Trading is accessible to almost all who are interested. Growth in companies of 20% or more a year is becoming more and more common. The old economy companies that rely on organic growth are no longer the engine of the stock market. Share prices that increase by 20% a year, even 100% a year are happening as we swim in a world of breakthroughs and disruptions.

Respect the market. If you are arrogant, the market will humble you. You will be proud of how you make honest money with your common sense and discipline. You will also relish making the money while having fun and excitement.

Chapter 20

Be Very Disciplined in Your Approach

When investing, being disciplined means following a process. It involves not being impulsive; not reacting on the spur of the moment; not being driven by a gambling mentality; not being emotional; not being affected by herd mentality; and not being overwhelmed by greed. It follows a process that is composed, rational and thoughtful. It is better to be slow and steady and to stay on course than to be hasty and veer off the road. Your sense of discipline is often revealed by the question: what have you done to arrive at the buying decision?

The process

If your process is right, then the result is more than likely to be right as well, whether it is stock picking or buying ETFs. Investing is not gambling. So good fortune does not depend on some lucky numbers, an auspicious day, or fate. Of course, we need a bit of luck in investing. But in a properly functioning market, in a well-managed country, luck has much less to do with it than following a thoughtful, disciplined process.

If a country is well managed, the economy should grow and do well and the stock market should grow. Take the US as an example: the S&P 500 has been growing at about 10% per year over the past decade, even faster in recent years. So, there is a pretty reasonable chance the investing outcome will be just as good.

So why be cute to try to time the market? Because you could end up buying high and selling low, not to mention paying unnecessary taxes and fees in the process. That's not to say you can't take advantage of dips and market corrections to buy assets that you have dreamed of owning at a good valuation.

Let's look at the US. The economy has been growing over the past several decades, despite the usual cycles, and even some major black swan events such as the 2008 Crash. The S&P has and looks to continue to grow, on average, by about 10% per year or even more for the foreseeable future. That is not to say there is not going to be a period of prolonged stagnation. From 1999-2009, the S&P return was -2%. However, this could be regarded as abnormal. Given a longer time horizon, the market will right itself to achieve the annual average return. It happened with Japan, which experienced the so-called Lost Decades (1991-2011), for very different reasons.

So, let's look at a couple of scenarios and the thought process a young retail investor may go through:

Illustration A: To buy an ETF-tracking S&P

The background and assumptions:

The US is still a capitalist nation that respects the rule of law, practices good corporate governance, and is at the forefront of innovation. Nothing has fundamentally changed and it is not foreseen to change drastically in the next few years.

So the market valuation is a bit rich and some companies are traded at a 'frothy' level.

In recent years interest rates have been extremely low and are forecast to remain low; therefore, holding bonds is not a good option.

Meanwhile, the inflation rate is creeping higher, thus eroding the value of money. So putting your cash to work and hedging its value is the way to go.

Other regions' historical performance has on average been less attractive than the US and have also been more unpredictable.

Low transaction costs matter, so ETF investing seems to fit the bill; what's more, the ETFs historical performance over the long term has not proven to yield any less than the actively managed mutual funds.

The S&P consists of 500 of the largest companies in the US. It has increased by about 10% per year on average over the past few decades.

There is still a lot of cash sloshing around in the economy. The savings rate for the country has also gone up to a historical high. So, demand for equity is likely to remain strong.

The retail investor has read up a bit about investing and understands the concept of dollar-cost averaging.

After graduating, the young investor has just received their first paycheck. Having reflected on the above information, their brain is telling them to play it safe because they have little disposable income. They trust the US economy which has proven itself a good investment for the past decade; they are happy with the above-inflation rate of return; moreover, there is no alternative even close to it, in terms of risk-reward return. They are young and can wait out bad cycles and they do not want to pay too much overhead to anyone because they understand that this will accumulate over time. They have heard and read a lot about ETFs and how they have become a very popular investment product. They have heard many savvy and well-known investors singing their praises and recognise that it is a very good way to invest.

So they have Googled for an index fund that tracks the S&P and found a few very large and well-established ones that have been established for several years and charge extremely low expenses. They expect an historical return of 10% or more for these ETFs.

Now they are ready to start their first investment. They know they have not been rash. They know that over time, if their country does not fail them, they should soon be smiling broadly.

Illustration B - To buy a company stock (also see Stock Picking)

The macro picture is positive, nothing on the horizon suggests that the economy is going to tank any time soon. Experienced professional investors and multi-billion-dollar portfolio managers come on air to talk about the market, the economic cycle, and to present their thoughts on stock recommendations. They put their reputation on the line by making recommendations in international news forums. They present their arguments which are then debated and challenged by their peers. The moderators constantly challenge the arguments presented to make sure public information does not mislead their viewer investors.

The retail investor then follows up on the proposed investments by verifying the target company's financial statements, which contain the key financials. The financials confirm that revenue and earnings growth have been good. The company CEO and CFO are interviewed on TV to shed more light on the company. Investors have a chance to assess their character and ability, and by extension, that of the management team

On the brokerage platform, it is shown that most analysts and research houses have given "buy" or "outperform" ratings for the stock.

The company has reported significant growth in the past few years and the last few quarters. Guidance for the company is for this trend to continue. The stock prices have increased significantly as a result.

The company is a household name. Its products are ubiquitous, with more promising products in the pipeline.

Now, looking at the share price and its valuation, it is indeed not excessive, because the PE is reasonable and inexpensive compared to its peers.

The research houses have set target prices of 10-20% above the current level.

The price of the stock can sometimes dip after the purchase, like any other stock. However, given its earnings growth, the long-term prospects should be sound.

So the investor, thinks to themself: "The world is doing ok, the country is doing ok, the economy is doing ok. They now hear the recommendation from the smart professionals on this stock, and start to wonder - they can't all be wrong, surely?" They check the financials and have found that indeed, the company is fundamentally great (a large company, huge profit, phenomenal growth in revenue and profit, etc)! They look around, the products are being used by everyone, households and business enterprises; they have become almost indispensable, and the brand has become the go-to brand.

Each step of this thought process has been thoughtful and methodical; more common sense than technical. So now the investor starts to dip their toe into the water. Instead of buying the full amount with their savings, they will buy one-third of it first. As it dips a bit more, they will buy a bit more again. During the three to six months after the purchase, the stock could dip below the original purchase price. But if the thesis remains intact, they should expect to see the stock price starting to move above the purchase price, driven among other things, by the earnings growth in the coming quarters.

So this is how the game is played.

Chapter 21

Common Sense Is Not Beyond You

Retail investors are not often trained in the very technical and financial aspects of the investment world. The good news is that sound investing does not depend solely on sophisticated analysis. You don't have to be a Formula One driver to drive well and safely. Observing traffic rules, driving defensively, having a safe car, and being sober will get you to your destination better and faster than an overconfident professional. A good measure of common sense, good discipline, and some basic financial knowledge, and a constant defensive posture will stand you in good stead. In fact, a professional who is too narrowly focused on technical and fundamental analysis could totally miss out on an opportunity, or even make the wrong call.

Common sense, practical judgment and a basic ability to perceive and judge is not the preserve of the professionals or the highly educated. Everyone can possess a measure of common sense and sound judgement. It comes from reading widely, interacting with smart people, and learning from them. Some principles are very simple and based on the day-to-day logic that we encounter throughout our lives. Often self-improvement comes from applying the same principles of good practice, over and over again, until it becomes normal behaviour.

Take buying a property, as an example. We know that a good property has to suit the purpose of the purchaser; it should be situated in a good location; be well managed (if it's a condominium); be structurally flawless and have aesthetic appeal. Before buying the property we do our due diligence; consult with qualified people who can provide different perspectives; and of course, make sure it is being sold at a reasonable price. We evaluate if it is a good price by comparing it with similar houses and reviewing a few statistics. For example, a property that is fetching a rental of $10k per month should theoretically be worth twice the price of one that only fetches $5k, all things being equal. In stock picking parlance, we use the price-earnings ratio (the PE ratio). A company that earns more deserves a higher share price than a company that earns less (see Chapter 23 - Making sense of financial statements).

Applying the same common sense to investing, we first of all want to invest in the best countries, the best companies, the best sectors, and the best products. We want them to make the most money and grow the fastest without being careless. Therefore, we expect them to be run by the best leaders and the best workforce. Fortunately, a lot of this information on the best companies can be found online. In fact, they should already be global household names, in your country or region. We would not want to buy anything that we know nothing about. If we are familiar with the territory, we can make better sense of it all; we can better appreciate how good their products and services are. They are most likely to be in the news frequently, so we can, in a way, monitor their progress.

Whatever we purchase, we want to know how others rate the product. If most of the independent rating houses are giving it 'buy' or 'outperform' ratings, that would be a sufficiently good reference. So much of the thinking has already been done for us. We only have to understand the background to their recommendations, and make sure the purchase is suitable for our portfolio and our situation.

As young investors still building up knowledge and experience, we do not want to be too adventurous. So we dip our toes in and test the water before taking the plunge. Have respect for the water, don't go into the deep end of the pool until you are ready. It is just common sense.

There is no need to be cute about interpreting the market's every move, buying and selling stocks and rotating in and out of sectors. Buying lesser-known stocks which are rarely covered by analysts should also be avoided. With common sense, we should be able to differentiate a lot of the noise from the facts. There are often conflicting opinions aired by the most seasoned professionals. The ability to see through all of that, filtering out irrelevant information is key to making a balanced decision.

The simple formula is to find investments that are good for now and the foreseeable future and hold on to them until they have changed fundamentally and no longer look so convincing.

Let's look at a scenario to illustrate:

Oil stocks have not been doing well over the last four or five years. However, there have been some news reports that the oil sector will begin to outperform for the next six months. This is due to supply constraint resulting from under-investment and an economy that is re-opening after the global pandemic. The oil boom is expected to continue for a few years until the transition into renewables.

At the moment, the price is already up more than 40% to $70/barrel. Professionals believe that the oil prices could go up even more.

We know that oil stock prices depend on a few unpredictable factors: weather, season, economic cycle, OPEC cartel price-fixing, geopolitics, supply disruption, ESG trends, government policies, etc. Oil company stock prices are heavily correlated to oil prices.

The recent trend in the Energy sector is towards ESG products (environmental, social and corporate governance) and renewables. Oil stocks used to be a bigger portion of the overall market; it has since dwindled to less than 5%. Long term, fossil fuels are said to be out of favour and the prospect for oil stocks is very uncertain. Many traders admit that buying oil stock is more for short-term trading, not a long-term hold.

As a comparison, the S&P is returning 10% annually for the past few years and is expected to continue growing at that rate. The mega-tech sector has offered phenomenal returns over the past few years (on average about 30%) and the trend is expected to continue. Each of these large cap stocks is a monolith, often as big as the entire GDP of a country. The analysts unanimously consider these sectors to be core holdings in their portfolio and a long-term hold.

Here are the common-sense things to consider:

How much higher do we think oil prices will go up? Maybe to $100, which is at a multi-year high? So how much higher do we expect the stock prices to go up by? By another 30-40%? When would that be?

Are we able to monitor the oil prices with confidence and get the timing right? Do we want to be glued to the screen constantly watching the price?

Let's say that the alternative is to buy one of the mega-tech stocks, which we know have a consistent return of 30% per year. Over a few years, can we say the oil stocks will provide a better return than the mega-tech stocks?

The common-sense question should be: is 30% on average return over the last five years not good enough? Should you take a gamble that oil prices will go up to $100/barrel? Would we also be able to tolerate the risk of oil prices tumbling to $30/barrel which happened pre-pandemic. How much oil stock do we have to buy to make it significant enough in our portfolio to move the dial and yet not carry a disproportionate risk? Do we think we can better understand and monitor the oil market or their business better than other household names like the mega-tech? Is it even worth spending the time if their significance is relatively small?

Let's assume we have $100k of assets. We allocate 5% of this to the bet on oil stocks to take advantage of the in-favour oil sector. Let's say a good return for it would be a 100% return in a year. We would be very happy if we achieved that, i.e. a return of $5k, which is only 5% of the portfolio; hardly enough to move the needle. One should not count on this to be repeated the next year and beyond. If this is invested instead in a mega-tech stock, the expected return would be 30% or more, as shown historically. This return is expected to be repeated for at least the next few years. If we bet on the oil stocks, we want to time it well to 1) buy the oil stocks at the right time, 2) dispose of them at the right time, and 3) get back to buying the mega-tech stocks at the right time.

Let's say by then the mega-tech stock has gone up by 30%. In effect, the gain from the oil stock is only 70% (100% - 30%). For retail investors to get all this timing right is not easy. If you get it wrong, you could lose 50% of the oil stock investment, as opposed to 30% or more gain from the mega-tech stock, a return expected to be repeated for at least the next few years. Look at your situation and find the option most appropriate for you.

Let's look at another situation:

You are fully invested in a balanced portfolio. Your current portfolio of $100k is well planned and balanced; made up of S&P tracking ETFs, some international ETFs, some mega-tech, and a small percentage of the more risky bets on disruptive technology.

Fixed income is unattractive because the yield is abysmal.

The US equity market has been returning about 10% annually over the past decades. You have high conviction in the performance of the IT sector, due to recent years' outperformance and excellent growth prospects.

You have cash in hand of $20k. You don't want it to sit in idle cash, because you fear that the dollar is being diluted as the government continues to print more money and the deficit is ballooning. You want to reduce it to $10k, i.e. to invest $10k.

You want to focus on the US. But the US indexes are already at almost all-time highs; according to the professionals. Every day you are bombarded with news of the market going higher, everywhere you turn, there is euphoria.

Some mega-tech stock prices have been going sideways for nine months due to various market jitters, even irrationality, despite reporting blowout earnings for the last two quarters. There is nothing on the horizon to suggest these earnings will not continue.

Many/most analysts are predicting the indexes will be higher by year-end (six months more).

So what do you do?

You could buy into a mega-tech stock since its valuation has become increasingly compelling. Buy less if you are less confident and extend the dollar-cost averaging from one week to over three months. You could also buy into the indexes using ETFs, as opposed to stock picking but do it using dollar-cost averaging. Since some of the mega-tech stock are already at an all-time high and could continue to grow as in the past decades, you could buy a smaller lot over a longer period, in this case, as little as $500 over the next 12 months. Of course, the lot size could be increased if a market correction becomes more pronounced.

Some of these mega-tech stocks are great to own, for so many good reasons. This is also why they are held by many institutional investors as core long-term holdings. We often lament how we have missed the early opportunities when the stock prices were very low. However, there will always be opportunities to buy in so that we own these great and rewarding stocks. While their stock prices tend to trend upward, there are times when the companies suffer a bit of hiccup, or the market perception has been misguided, resulting in their prices being corrected. So, a healthy dose of 'fear of missing out' (FOMO) is probably healthy. Start to nibble when every little window of opportunity arises. Otherwise, you will never own any of these great stocks, thereby missing out entirely, and missing the golden years of their explosive growth.

There are more nuances in real life but this example illustrates how applying simple concepts will moderate your risk, giving you a much better chance of making money over the long run.

May common sense prevail.

Chapter 22
Setting Goals and Monitoring Progress

The following steps are broadly what is required to implement a successful investing strategy:

- Look at and understand the various investment types and their past performances and risk profiles.

- Define your portfolio based on your risk-reward profile.

- Based on the past performance and desired portfolio, project the targeted returns for the next 10, 20, 30 years.

- Monitor the progress of the investments through the investment horizon, make adjustments to the investments as and when necessary to meet the goals.

Assuming that we have now acquired some basic knowledge of the various investment types (see Chapter 11 on 'Understand major investment types') we decide that we want to invest in the broader market (instead of individual company stock), more in line with our risk tolerance. We also decide that we want to achieve a decent, consistent, return over time.

To understand how the broader markets have been performing, we can look at the major indexes. These indexes have hundreds of companies represented and are therefore relatively well-diversified. See Illustration 31 below that shows the performance of some of the major indexes in the US and other regions:

Illustration 31 – Performance of major indexes

Market	Annualized Returns		
	1 Year	**5 years**	**10 years**
S&P	56.5%	16.3%	13.9%
S&P small cap	96.0%	15.6%	13.0%
Nasdaq	70.6%	28.2%	20.2%
Dow	59.6%	16.7%	13.9%
Health care	39.6%	14.9%	16.0%
Europe	49.0%	8.8%	5.5%
Emerging	57.0%	11.7%	3.4%
China	27.2%	9.4%	3.0%
India	29.3%	16.4%	13.5%

Note: The data above was extracted during the time of the writing and could have since changed. Some data was based on ETFs tracking the particualr index. The table is for reference and illustrative purposes only. Any purchasing of the products should refer to the latest official documents.

The statistics above show that the major US indexes have been returning more than 10% per year on average, while other countries and continents have lagged. While past performances are no guarantee of future performances, they could be a good reference for the future, especially of the developed economies with a long-proven record. So based on their proven track record, it is possible to quantify our expected future returns.

Define our portfolio based on our risk-reward profile

We now know the return percentage of each of the broad investment types, based on their past performance. We also know what risks they carry. With this knowledge, we can now formulate our investment portfolio – see Chapter 14 on 'Sound portfolio management'.

Let's say the investments below reflect our portfolio:

Investment	Portfolio ratio
S&P (VOO)	30.0%
Nasdaq (VGT)	20.0%
Big Tech	10.0%
Europe	10.0%
IWDA	10.0%
Emerging	10.0%
Bond	5.0%
Cash	5.0%
Total	100.0%

This portfolio mostly invests in low-expense funds, each of which holds shares in hundreds of companies. It is more weighted toward the US and in technology but also diversifies to take advantage of other international, developed, and emerging markets. It is pretty well-diversified while also taking advantage of the better-performing markets.

Based on historical returns and the desired portfolio, it is now possible to roughly target your expected returns. This is not a wild stab in the dark but a logical extrapolation of the past into the future.

The question may be asked, 'Why rely on past performance for the forecast?' Firstly, if the structure of the country and market has remained strong and the structure undergoes yearly inspection, its past performance should be expected to continue. Secondly, the track record has been proven over a long period.

Based on the portfolio above and setting the targets from the very beginning of the investing journey, the targeted returns from the portfolio would be 8.15% per year (before tax).

Illustration 32 - Projected returns based on desired portfolio

Investment	*Past 10 Years' Annual Returns	Target Expected Annual Returns	Portfolio Ratio	Portfolio Allocation ($)	Target Annual Portfolio Returns ($)
S&P (VOO)	13.9%	10.0%	30.0%	3,000	300
Nasdaq (VGT)	20.2%	12.0%	20.0%	2,000	240
Big Tech		15.0%	10.0%	1,000	150
Europe	5.5%	3.0%	10.0%	1,000	30
IWDA		6.0%	10.0%	1,000	60
Emerging	3.4%	3.0%	10.0%	1,000	30
Bond		1.0%	5.0%	500	5
Cash	0.0%	0.0%	5.0%	500	-
Total			100.0%	10,000	815

*Assumed reference numbers for illustrative purposes only.

Targeted Overall Portfolio Return (Total 'Targeted Annual Portfolio Returns'/Total 'Portfolio Allocation ($)')	**8.15%**

If this expected return is deemed too low, the retail investor may choose to take on more risk for a higher return, e.g. by investing in more growth stocks, or more ETFs that invest in disruptive technology (for example the ETF tech funds) with the promise of a higher return. So, in a way, we already have a good idea of our expected investment returns. The reality may be different as it unfolds but we would know the reasons for the deviation when we compare the actual returns with the expected returns.

Even if we engage an advisor to help us manage the investment, it is equally important to know and set our targeted returns, so that we are in a better position to make sure the advisors are performing as expected.

With the targeted percentage return, you can now project your investment 10, 20, 30 years into the future. We will know, from the outset, how many years it will take us to reach our goals. So, let's say we want to accumulate asset value to a certain amount by the time we hit a certain age. We are now in a position to see if our projection will pan out. It may show that the expectation is unrealistic; or have a good chance of being met; or something in between. Corrective actions can then be formulated to guide it closer to the expected outcome.

Investment is a long-term exercise. It could be anything from 10 years to 30 years, or even become cross-generational. At the outset, there are many routes in front of us leading to very different outcomes. Some routes, in fact, will take us backward (loss-making) instead of forward to where we want to get to. To only realise your mistakes at the end of the long journey will truly be a tragic outcome. Remember to monitor the progress of your investments through the investment horizon and make adjustments to the investments, as and when necessary, to meet your goals.

When the portfolio has deviated from the plan, as shown in the table below, actions can be taken to bring it back in line. Such deviations occur frequently due to the constant changes in the values of each component investment, or as fresh money comes into the portfolio. See Illustration 33 below.

Illustration 33 – Portfolio summary, plan and deviation

Category	Investment	Planned Portfolio %	Planned Portfolio ($)	Actual Portfolio ($)	Deviation from Plan ($)
Index	US - S&P	20%	4,000	9,500	5,500
Index	US - Small cap	15%	3,000	-	(3,000)
Index	US - IT (Nasdaq)	20%	4,000	-	(4,000)
Sector/stock	US - IT stock	5%	1,000	7,500	6,500
Sector/stock	US - Heath care stock	5%	1,000	-	(1,000)
Sector/stock	US - Other stock(energy/other)	5%	1,000	-	(1,000)
Type	Bond	5%	1,000	1,000	0
Geography	Europe	8%	1,600	-	(1,600)
Geography	Asia (China/India/Japan/Korea/Other)	10%	2,000	-	(2,000)
Geography	Emerging (ex Asia)	2%	400	1,000	600
Type	Other	5%	1,000	1,000	0
Total		100%	20,000	20,000	0

The targeted future returns and asset value are necessarily based on estimates and assumptions. Being estimates and forecasts, there could be potential upside or downside to the numbers, thereby providing more tailwind or headwind to reaching your end goal. When the returns deviate from your plan, actions can be taken to stay on course. That these goals are set in numbers makes them more real – what gets measured gets done. We will be more motivated to stick to them. The figures are not based on some lucky numbers, or burning of joss sticks, or auspicious occurrences; they are cold, hard numbers!

For many, after years of working, saving up and investing, assets will have been accumulated in different forms, in different locations, under different names. They could be in cash tucked under the mattress; deposits in obscure tax-efficient jurisdictions; investments in nominee accounts; properties in different exotic locations; stocks held in various brokerage platforms; or jewellery in safe-deposit boxes away from prying eyes. In other words, they could be in many different forms in many different places.

At the end of all the hard work, we want to know the progress of our hard-earned investing. Have our overall assets been growing at the pace we expected? Or are they being depleted even as we are working hard, saving hard, and investing the best we can? If we know we are making more than expected, we may loosen the belt and pamper ourselves and our loved ones a little bit more, but always keeping our eyes on the long-term goal. We cannot spend with abandonment without knowing how far we are from our end goal.

Brokerage platforms usually provide reports that summarize the performances of the accounts held with them. If you have multi-assets invested across various channels, an Excel summary would help to give a quick overview of all the assets. So all the assets owned are brought under one umbrella.

See Illustration 34 below for a simple example of a summary that only requires a few minutes to update at end of each month, or as and when desired. Here, in one glance, we know how much wealth has been accumulated and the changes from one period to the next and over the long investing journey.

The change in the asset value could be compared with the original targets set, and against the broader market indicators. For example, if the target set was 8.2%

per year (see Illustration 33 above), and the S&P has achieved 10%. We want to understand where our actual performances have fallen short, and if necessary, take the necessary corrective actions.

Illustration 34 - Monthly asset summary

Asset ($K)	2020	2021											
	Dec	Jan	Feb	Mar	Apr	May	Jun	Jul	Aug	Sep	Oct	Nov	Dec
Properties	200	200	200	200	200								
Wealthfront	125	130	132	128	135								
Robinhood	80	80	75	75	80								
401K	175	180	185	175	190								
HSA	14	14	14	14	14								
Employee stock	195	200	195	190	205								
Cash	11	13	10	13	13								
Other													
Total	**800**	**817**	**811**	**795**	**837**	-	-	-	-	-	-	-	-
Monthly % change		2.1%	-0.7%	-2.0%	5.3%								
YTD % change		2.1%	1.4%	-0.6%	4.7%								

Chapter 23
Making Sense of Financial Statements

The health of a company is to a large extent revealed through its financial statements. The main ones are the Profit and Loss Statement, the Balance Sheet, and the Cashflow Statement. Public companies are required to disclose all relevant information to the public, including their analysis of their strengths, weaknesses, opportunities, and threats, in other words, any information that may be of significant interest to the investors.

Through these financial statements, one can see if the company is making money, how strong it is as a company through the assets it holds and the liabilities it carries, and how much cash it is generating. The good thing is that it is not beyond us to be educated on the basics, although a short course in accounting will also be helpful.

Financial statements and information for public companies can usually be found on the company's website under Investor Relations. These include quarterly and annual reports. It is also made available on many of the brokerage platforms in their research functionality. It is usually in a summarized form that contains the key financial indicators, past, present and forecast.

The research functionality may also include access and links to reports by other professional research firms (for example, CFRA, Argus) that provide the analysis on the target companies. These reports usually also include the key financials, their analysis and interpretation to arrive at their views.

Instead of reading through the thick reports published by the target companies, which could overwhelm an average retail investor, referring to these summarized financials as well as the analysis, would in many cases suffice for making informed and fast investment decisions.

The Profit and Loss Statements

A business operates primarily to make a profit for its shareholders, unless it is a charitable organization. A company that does not make money will have difficulty surviving and will eventually be wound up. When this happens, the shareholders will lose any money they have invested in the company. So the Profit and Loss Statement will show how much revenue the company has generated and how much profit it is making during a certain period.

See Illustration 35 below for a simple template of the P&L Statement.

Description	$	Explanations
Sales revenue	100,000	Revenue from sales of products and services
Less:		
Cost of Goods Sold	60,000	Cost of goods that are either manufactured or purchased and then sold
Gross Profit	40,000	Profit made after subtracting the cost of goods sold from the revenue
Gross Margin	40%	
Less:		
Selling and Administrative Expenses	10,000	All everyday operating expenses of running a business, and includes nearly all business costs not covered in the category of cost of goods sold
Net Operating Profit	30,000	Profit from a company's primary or core business operations after all expenses are taken out except for the cost of debt, taxes, and certain one-off items
Other Income/ (expenses)	-	Income not from the company's main business
Net Profit before tax	30,000	Earnings after subtracting all expenses but before tax
Income Tax (30%)	9,000	Tax the company pays on its profit
Net Profit/(Loss) after tax	21,000	Total earnings after subtracting all expenses

No one wants to pay too much for a stock, no matter how much they love it. If the stock price of a company is low it does not necessarily mean it is 'cheap'. A company could do a stock split, thereby reducing its stock price to a fraction of what it was before, without any change to its fundamental value. So, for example, the fact that Apple's stock price is $125 per unit while Amazon's is $3,000 does not mean that Amazon is too expensive or that Apple is dirt cheap.

So what is considered "paying too much" for a stock? By this, we are talking about the valuation of the stock; or the price paid by investors based on its ability to make money. The higher the price, the more money it should make. Otherwise, this metric would indicate that the stock is overpriced. So, if we buy a stock for $100 per share and it is earning $2 per share, that means it will take 50 years ($100/$2) to recoup our money. If the company is making $10 per year instead of just $2, it will take only 10 years ($100/$10). If the company is not making any money, mathematically it just means you would never recoup your initial investment ($100/$0).

PE Ratio

One commonly-used measure of a stock's valuation is the Price Earnings ratio (PE), i.e. the share price/earnings per share (EPS) for the year. EPS is the earnings/number of shares of a company. The PE is, therefore, dependent on three factors:

1. The stock price

Stock prices could go up or down every second the stock market is trading. The price of a stock will depend on various factors, including the company's fundamentals and market conditions.

2. Company earnings

Earnings in simple terms refer to the profit made by companies. Companies make money by selling products or providing services above their costs. In a market economy, companies exist primarily to make a profit for their shareholders. This profit may be distributed to investors (normally as a dividend) or retained by the company for future use.

3. Number of shares

Companies can issue more shares or reduce the number of shares through a buyback; both actions have the effect of decreasing or increasing the earnings per share of the company, as earnings of the company will be shared by more or less of the shareholders' base. By buying back its own stock, a company is also signalling to the market that it views the current price as too low and is worth buying, thereby also boosting market confidence. Companies that are in a position to buy back their stock are those that generate a lot of profit and cash, another positive signal to the market. For example, Apple has the habit of buying back billions of dollars of its stock and has indicated its intention to continue to do so in the future, a positive signal for its ongoing share price.

So, a high PE could mean the stock price has gone up too much relative to its earnings, or that the earnings have not kept pace with its share price. The stock price is, therefore, less attractive compared to one with a smaller PE.

A company with a track record of consistent, excellent, past performance will command a good stock price. Sometimes companies may not do as well presently but are forecast to do much better in the coming quarters. In this case, future estimates of the earnings are also used (referred to as Forward Earnings Estimates and Forward PE) to better reflect its earnings prospects. However, estimates are at best just estimates. Estimates more than a year into the future are less reliable for stock purchase decisions and should be used with caution. It is best to refer to consensus estimates by different reputable agencies to arrive at a majority consensus. These estimates by various independent sources are often available on your trading platform. Most companies will also provide forward guidance on their coming quarter's performance.

For an investor, paying a high price for a company not currently making any profit, and uncertain when it will in the future, carries substantial risks. You might be surprised but there are companies today that are trading at astronomical PE figures that are yet to make money. Some are due to the perceived prospects, often in their early days of a disruptive technology breakthrough or new business model. An example would be Amazon in its early days and Tesla currently. But there are others, simply due to the herd mentality of uninformed retail investors, following news unsubstantiated by facts. A careful evaluation of a company's current valuation prior to purchase is a must.

The Balance Sheet

The P&L tells us if a company is making money while the Balance Sheet (B/S) tells us the assets and liabilities of a company.

See Illustration 36 below for a simple Balance Sheet.

Balance Sheet of ABC Company as at 31 December 2020			
Fixed asset	600	Capital	1,000
		Retained earnings	200
Accounts Receivables	2,000		
Inventory	500	Account Payables	500
Cash	600	Bank loan	2,000
Total Assets	**3,700**	**Total Liabilities and Equity**	**3,700**

The balance sheet will always balance. How so? Let's use a simple scenario to illustrate. When the company started, it received cash from the shareholders. The shareholders' stake in the company is shown as a liability owed to the shareholders and cash in the bank as an asset. In other words, the balance sheet balances because **Assets = Liabilities + Equity**. When the company takes up a loan to purchase products for resale, it will show as a loan liability and inventory will show as an asset. So at the end of the accounting period, the balance sheet will show the company now has *liabilities* of paid-up capital and loan on one side; and on the other hand, *assets* of cash and inventory.

Where a company makes losses year after year, its assets are being depleted by the losses, weakening the balance sheet. Conversely, as profits are made year after year, the balance sheet will show total assets, which includes the all-important cash, that is greater than the total liabilities. So when the airlines were grounded for more than a year during Covid-19, with planes hardly flying, there was little revenue and enormous losses. Each month that planes are not flying means the prospect of an airline going bankrupt increases significantly, unless bailed out by the Government.

When the airlines finally started flying again due to higher vaccination rates, investors should know that the Balance Sheet of many airlines would already have been seriously degraded. So, while revenue may see a rebound, the airlines would be saddled with a lot of debts that will impact their future performance for years. Investors should be very careful about investing in airlines.

Retail investors will find it useful to at least have some understanding of the fundamentals of the Balance Sheet. This information is readily available online and not daunting to grasp. We should invest in companies that have a strong balance sheet that can weather all circumstances. As long-term investors, we invest in companies that can endure and prosper.

The Cashflow Statement

This statement is particularly important because it indicates how much cash has been generated by the company and its source. A profitable company may not generate enough cashflow to continue to operate. For example, it may have sold its products profitably but not been able to collect the proceeds critical for its operating expenses. A company choked-off from its cash flow dies a faster death than an unprofitable one. So, investors pay particular attention to the cash flow generated by a company in order to gauge its overall performance and viability.

The Cashflow Statement is prepared directly or indirectly. The direct method is easier. It records the cash received and the cash paid through its operating activities. Even a person untrained in accounting could understand it. The indirect method is a bit more technical. It is prepared by looking at the Income Statements and the Balance Sheet, adjusting for non-cash items and some items to reveal more of the flow of cash during the period. The Statement will reveal these cashflows:

- Cash from operating activities

- Cash from investing activities

- Cash from financing activities

A company that keeps borrowing money to finance its non-profitable operating activities is not viable in the long run. Companies that churn out tons of cash year-after-year are, of course, very desirable and command high stock prices. These are companies that are not only selling a lot of their product or services but are also very profitable and are realizing their profit in cash. With the cash, the companies can keep investing to lay more golden eggs, or return some to their shareholders as dividends or by buying back its stock. Both these activities will positively impact its stock price.

As a retail investor you should understand the meaning of each of the often-used terms. When the news and the professionals keep referring to them, you can then make more sense of their analysis.

Chapter 24
Brokerage/Trading Platforms

Choosing the right trading platform is important. A good platform offers a one-stop-shop for helping you pick, buy and hold the desired investment products. The main considerations in choosing a brokerage platform include efficient functionality; good service support; low trading fees and other fees; favourable exchange rates; access to global exchanges; real-time trading data; quality research information; and simple conditions to open an account.

A trading platform should provide these basic functions:

- Screening mechanism to select the desired investment products

- Extensive information for investment decisions

- Access to reports from independent agencies

- Access to real-time pricing

- Quality performance reports

- Facilitation of fund transfers

- Custody service for investment accounts, including facilitating payments for securities purchased, receiving dividends, and keeping the assets safe.

For example, a retail investor may be looking to invest in large-cap companies with high growth, profitability, good analyst ratings, and dividend yield. They can screen for this on their brokerage platform, specifying these criteria. The screener may throw up Apple (APPL) as a candidate. The retail investor can then drill down further into the company, which should show the key indicators at a glance, as follows:

Illustration 37 - Stock key financials

Description	Apple	Explanation
Market capitalization	2.1T	The total dollar market value of a company, by multiplying its stock's current market price by the total number of shares that can be bought and sold by the public.
Current price	$123	The most recent selling price of a stock
Dividend yield:	0.70%	Dividend paid out by a company expressed as a percentage of its share price. The formula is: divide the annual dividends paid per share by the price per share.
PE	28	Price-to-earnings ratio - measures the company's share price relative to its earnings per share
PE forward	24	Price-to-earnings ratio - measures the company's share price relative to its future estimated earnings per share
EPS		Earnings per share, calculated as a company's profit divided by the number of outstanding shares
Q1 2021	1.68	
Q2 2021	1.4	
Q3 2021 (est.)	1	
Q42021 (est.)	1.12	
2021 FY	5.2	
2022	5.2	
200-day moving average	$124	The average closing price of a stock over the last 200 days
Recent peak price (18/1/2021)	$145	
Rating by agencies:		Ratings assigned by analysts or rating agencies
CFRA	4 stars	The best is 5 stars
Argus	Buy	Ranges from buy, hold, to sell
Credit Suisse	Neutral	The stock is expected to perform in line with the expected returns of the market
Reuters	Outperform	Underperform - projected to do slightly worse than the market average, overperform - projected to provide returns higher than the market average
Target prices	$150-160	Analysts' projection of a stock's future price
Revenue growth		The increase, or decrease, in a company's sales between two periods
2021 (estimate)	24.9%	
2020	5.5%	
2019	-2.3%	
Earning growth		The increase, or decrease, in a company's earnings between two periods
2021 (estimate)	39.4%	
2020	3.9%	
2019	-7.8%	

Note: The data above was extracted during the time of the writing and could have since changed. The table is for reference and illustrative purposes only. Any purchasing of the products should refer to the latest official documents.

Different platforms offer trading of investment products in different domiciles. For example, Charles Schwab offers trading in stocks and ETFs mainly listed on the US exchanges. Interactive Brokers on the other hand trade on both the US and international exchanges. To open an account, many brokerages have certain conditions that investors must meet e.g. the requirement to maintain a minimum amount in the account.

Different brokerage platforms have different fee structures. They have become more and more competitive, to the point where some are offering to trade for no fee. Search online for comparisons of the fees charged by the brokerage platforms in your country.

The brokerages charge for a variety of services provided; for example, in addition to the trading fee, they may also charge a custodial fee (see Chapter 16 - Expenses matter), plus cost of currency conversion, etc. The way the fees are structured could affect some investors more than others because of the differences in investment style. For example, a trading fee may be charged on a per-trade basis or based on the transaction amount, or may be waived if a certain number of trades have been made during a certain period.

In the old days, a lot of trading activities were handled for retail investors by brokers. They also possessed the information important for investing decisions. Nowadays, however, trading can be done largely online by the retail investors themselves. The enormous advantage is that everything becomes controllable by the retail investors personally and instantaneously. With investment, speed is critical in any situation. Now anyone can trade anywhere, at any time, with little or no fees.

A suitable brokerage platform helps improve the performance of an investor's portfolio by:

- Providing accurate information to take advantage of opportunities

- Charging low and competitive fees

- Making available a wide variety of desired investment products

- Saving investors' time through its efficient functionality.

Chapter 25
Professional Advisors and Asset Management Services

Most of us are not professionals in investing; we just have surplus cash that we want to put to work to generate more wealth. It can be very easy to find ourselves overwhelmed by the investment world.

There is an array of options to help us manage our investible assets. Some of these options are:

- DIY (do-it-yourself)

- Engage professionals such as Financial Planners/Asset Managers/Wealth Managers

- Private banking

- Robo-advisors

Regardless of whether an investor decides to do it themselves, or engage the professionals, educating oneself with the basics of investing is important. Investors have to make sense of whatever they are investing in, including the investment made for them by the professionals.

As retail investors, we usually educate ourselves with some basic knowledge, then gain experience as we invest, sometimes learning lessons the hard way. If we just have a few thousand dollars to invest, then engaging a professional would seem to be overkill and the expenses hard to justify. A better choice would be to buy mutual funds through the banks and brokerages, or purchase ETFs and stocks online.

Start trading with small amounts, playing it safe by buying the bigger blue-chip or mega-tech companies with a solid track record. Get a feel for how it all hangs together by applying the basic knowledge that you have learned. Get familiar with your trading platform and the information available for investment decisions. Sometimes we can get too confident after making a few gains, thinking "I am really good at this". Even professionals have been taught many bitter lessons. So, be warned.

As retail investors, we tend to fly alone, sometimes in the dark and sometimes down the wrong path. If we want to handle our investments by ourselves, then at least listen and learn. To be equipped, have the cable business news run as much as possible throughout the day (for example CNBC, Bloomberg) as you multi-task. If this is too much work, try it out for a month or two; you may be surprised how much you learn. Or listen to the podcasts (for example CNBC- Fast Money and Half Time).

If you engage an advisor you probably won't get much time with them unless they are managing significant sums for you. The best you can hope for is a quarterly portfolio review and the odd phone call. If you have been keeping yourself up to date with the latest financial information, then you will at least be able to have a much more constructive discussion when you do actually meet.

As your portfolio gets bigger, the tax, risk management, and administrative issues could become more complicated and overwhelming. It may then be time to engage the services of a professional. The peace of mind they offer, the expertise in risk protection, the tax optimization, the administrative chores, could all justify the expenses and fees paid. Moreover, their active management in a stock-pickers market could help you outperform the market.

The fees of many professionals have become more competitive in recent years due to the rise of online platforms. The management fee charged by an Asset Manager may on average be 1%, but the range could be between 0.5-2%. The fee also depends on the style of the asset management, the size of the asset under management, etc. The fees tend to be lower if the style is more passive investing than active. The more tailor-made and more human interactions that are required, the higher will be the fee. The bigger the asset amount, the more the fee rate becomes negotiable. Not only should an investor ask of the fee paid, "What am I paying for?" but perhaps even more importantly, "Is what I am paying for what I am looking for?" (i.e. to complement or to plug the hole in your investment skillset). For example, if an investor is looking for advisors who will provide the latest stock-picking tips, advisors that work more on a discretionary mandate (i.e. leave the investing decision to the advisors) are unlikely to be suitable.

If you are a big fish, with tens of millions of investments, the case for working with professional advisors becomes more compelling. You have so much more to lose, not just because of poor tax planning but also from missed investment opportunities.

Advisors often work on a "discretionary mandate", meaning they invest your money the best way they can, based on their personal discretion. While they do try their best, they are only human, and could err in their investment judgment. There may be times when interests of the investors and advisors are not aligned. One of the biggest mistakes an investor could make is to entrust their funds to the advisors unquestioningly, thinking "they know best". Most of all, do not assume that all advisors will discharge their fiduciary duty as an ethical requirement. Investors who are clueless and not bothered to even understand the basics are themselves a significant risk. Over time, the difference in the end result could be heaven and earth.

Paying the fees for professional advice does not necessarily mean that they will outperform the passively managed ETFs. In fact, it has been proven by the historical performance that it is difficult for them to consistently outperform the passive funds – see Chapter 16 - Expenses Matter.

If you do decide to hire a professional, make sure that you get the best fees with the best and most trusted service possible. Always make sure you understand their recommendations and portfolio structure and take responsibility for your own decisions. At the very least, monitor the performance by constantly measuring it against the market. For example, as a simple yardstick, expect your returns to be in line with the market movements of the S&P and other indexes. After all, investors could easily DIY by investing in ETFs that track the S&P and other major indexes.

Somewhere between the low fees of ETFs and the higher fees for professional advice, there is another option – Robo-advisors. The futuristic-sounding tools have broken down some of the traditional barriers for the average retail investor. With these online, semi-automised platforms, sound financial planning is now accessible to everyone, not just high-net-worth individuals. Some of the well-known players in this are Vanguard Personal Advisor Service, Wealthfront, Betterment.

These digital platforms provide automated investment services driven by algorithms based on modern portfolio theory with little to no human supervision. They work by first gathering information on a client and then automatically investing for the client based on that data, mainly through the use of passive index investing strategies. They then continue to monitor and rebalance the portfolios to ensure optimal performance returns as set out in the mandate.

Robo-advisors are often very inexpensive and require very low opening balances to make them easily accessible to almost any investor. Because of the use of algorithms to automate trades and indexed ETF strategies, there is not a lot of human interaction with the professionals, which is why the cost is normally lower than that charged by the human advisors. Typically, they charge a flat annual fee of 0.2 to 0.5%, on the total account balance. That compares with the typical rate of 1% to 2% charged by a human financial planner.

Robo-advisors are also more accessible due to the ease of online access and are typically available 24/7. Furthermore, it takes significantly less capital to get started while human advisors would in many cases only take on new clients with investible assets in excess of $100,000.

Robo-advisors are best suited for straightforward investing and are not the best options for more complex issues, such as estate planning. This may limit the options for an individual investor. You cannot choose which mutual funds, ETFs, stocks, or bonds to invest in your account. Being an automated service, it is also ill-equipped to deal with unexpected crises or extraordinary situations.

A lot has changed in recent years for retail investors. Opening an account with an online brokerage platform has never been easier. These platforms are connected worldwide and enable trading stocks and securities almost anywhere in the world 24/7. Investment information is online and real-time and on brokerage platforms. There is cable news that feeds the latest global market info around the clock. Podcasts that let investors listen to subjects of interest at a convenient time. There are also Robo-advisory services that charge a lower fee (0.3-0.5%) by using smart algorithms to manage portfolios. The popularity of ETFs has also meant diversified portfolios at lower expense and are tradeable like stocks on the brokerage platform without going through any intermediaries. So almost everyone can take investment matters into their own hands.

Let's look at a situation to illustrate the thoughts in deciding if engaging an advisor is for you:

Let's say you have an asset of $100k; your advisor fee is 1% on the asset value, which

If you had bought an ETF tracking the S&P 500 then the fees charged by the fund companies would be 0.03% (for example VOO). You could buy this ETF on the brokerage platform and pay no other agency /brokerage fee or trading fee (with many platforms). So your fees/expenses are almost nil.

Now, the advisor, working on a discretionary mandate, may decide that buying ETF tracking the S&P is a good investment. After all, a historical return of 10% by the ETF is hard to beat. It would seem, in this case, the advisor appears to provide little incremental value, except a confirmation of your own opinion, and some psychological comfort.

You may think 1% the advisor charges is no big deal – it is! Let's assume the S&P returns 10%, let's also assume also the capital gains tax is 20% in your country, your 10% returns now become 7%. So, this is what you take home from your investment. Now, if the cost of living has gone up by 2% during the year (i.e. the inflation), your net cash generated in the year would be 5%. This return for taking the risk investing in equity may be adequate compensation and good enough in increasing your long-term wealth. Bear in mind 10% is a pretty good year; the market could often be worse.

Let's assume the ETF did not return 10% but instead only 5% ($5k). So capital gains of $5k will be offset with 1% of advisor fee ($1k), and capital gains of 20% on

$50k ($1k), giving you a net return of $3k, which equates to 3% return. If inflation is 2%, you had not been rewarded at all for bearing the risk of investing in equity.

Let's take the above situation further. Let's assume that the advisor for whatever reason, at their discretion, decides that instead of investing in the passive ETFs, you should buy actively-run mutual funds where the fund manager charges 1% of the annual management fee. Assuming the fund performs as well as the ETF (historically not many can consistently beat the markets) to return 10%, the net return after advisor fee of 1%($1k), fund management fee of 1%($1k), capital gains tax of 20% on the gains ($2k) dwindles to 6% ($6k). What if it had been a not-so-good year? What if the fund manager and the advisor had charged more than 1% each because you never bothered to check? Note that the fees are charged on the total amount of assets managed, not just the gains, in a profitable year as well as loss-making years. So, the impact of these fees is more accentuated in bad years; see Chapter 16 - Expenses Matter.

You should determine if the impact of the costs on your investment return is acceptable before engaging an advisor. Otherwise, it could well end up that everyone in this financial food chain is making money except you. $1k of advisory fees may sound like a lot to you, but the advisor who might have dozens of clients to serve, is unlikely to be able to afford more face time with individual clients. You may be offered one of their packages, categorized into a "conservative", "balanced", or "aggressive" portfolio. To reduce the burden of the advisory fee, perhaps the compromise to this is to have a portion of the $100k invested in the core assets that you will hold for the long term, leaving others to the advisors to manage; in this example, maybe $20-50k could go into index-tracking ETFs and the rest into other instruments for more diversification or seeking higher returns.

What is illustrated above is, be thoughtful of what you are trying to achieve by engaging the help of advisors. Many of them perform well and offer critical services but at a cost. If you do not have any professional help, do you know what you are doing? Decide on your level of comfort then decide which method works best for you.

Chapter 26

Have Adequate Insurance Coverage

Accidents and misfortune befall all of us to varying degrees during our long lives, often due to factors beyond our control. No matter how careful we are and how hard we try to avoid them, they will happen and can often cause untold disruption to our lives. To minimize the financial burden when these risks do happen, we could consider buying protection, in the form of insurance coverage.

The insurance industry has existed for many decades to cater to these needs. Typically, one party will take out an insurance policy with the insurance company by paying a regular premium, and in return, the insurance company will make a certain amount of payout to the party nominated by the policyholder to be the beneficiary in the event of the risk happening.

The insurance companies work out the premium to charge for a particular type of insurance coverage. Obviously, the higher the perceived risk, the higher the chances of the insurance company having to pay out, and the higher will be the premium charged. The most basic considerations in buying insurance coverage are: What or who should be insured against what kind of risks, and for how much?

There is usually insurance for almost any foreseeable risk. Where they are not available, it could be because there is a law against it, or the insurance companies deemed them uninsurable due to their immeasurable risks, rendering them too risky for the insurers.

The risks to be covered are explicitly spelled out in the insurance policy. It is crucial that the insurance buyer understands and makes sure that all the intended risk coverage is reflected in the insurance policy.

Be sure to evaluate the adequacy of the insurance coverage regularly because risk exposures change over time; what was adequate when the insurance policy was first written may no longer be adequate just a short time into the future.

With the best of intentions, some oversights do occur, or not all risks can be foreseen, or explicitly spelled out, or occasionally, there may be a total freak risk. Were this to happen, insurance may defer to the court for decision, thereby delaying or casting in doubt any hoped-for payout.

Watch those exclusion clauses. Insurance buyers often do not read the terms of agreement carefully and could be caught totally off guard. For example, a policy may state that it covers accidents but exclude a certain type of accident; or it covers sickness but excluding a certain type of sickness. So if you are particularly prone to a certain type of accident due to your career, or a particular sickness due to your lifestyle or family history, then exclusions by the insurance company will seriously defeat the purpose of the insurance. Read the fine print!

Everyone has different risk profiles because we all have different situations. These risks could happen to a person, their family, or their assets. The damage could be inflicted by an accident, sickness, loss of life, loss of earning capacity, loss of heath, natural disaster, man-made failures, etc. But there are some insurance types common in many countries. Three of them are:

1. Life insurance

The insurance company will pay death benefits to the named beneficiaries upon an insured person's death.

Who needs life insurance? Put simply, anyone with dependents. Dependents could be anyone financially dependent on the insured person. This could include parents, children, siblings, parents.

There are two major choices:

1. Term life insurance, which lasts a certain number of years, then ends. The insuring party could choose the term when taking out the policy. The common terms are 10, 20, or 30 years.

2. Permanent life insurance covers the insured's entire life unless the policyholder stops paying the premiums or surrenders the policy.

How much to insure for? One of the main considerations is how much is the desired payout by the insurance company to replace the income lost as a result of the death. So if the death of the person results in the loss of annual income of $50k and this amount is deemed the amount to sustain life as before, then the coverage will have to ensure payout annually of $50k, with adjustment for inflation in the subsequent years.

If the death occurs when there is debt to be settled of $50k, then the insurance coverage that ensures a payout of at least $50k will be appropriate.

If a person has enough wealth to pass down to the dependents, they probably won't need life insurance.

2. Disability insurance

A person's income may be lost due to disability. This could cause financial difficulties for the income earner and their dependents. This insurance seeks to compensate for the lost income caused by a disability. This may be purchased through the government in some countries but it can also be obtained through private insurers.

There are conditions to satisfy before qualifying for the compensation. The applicant has to satisfy the definition of disability in the context of this insurance and demonstrate that they can no longer continue in the same line of work in which they were previously engaged. The medical history may be reviewed. There is usually a waiting period before the applicant can be classified as disabled, the amount of income is replaced, and confirmation received concerning the length of time that the benefits will continue to be paid.

3. Homeowner's insurance

Our home is not only where we shelter our families, it is often also one of our largest investments. It represents many years of love and sweat. So we want to make sure we keep it indefinitely for ourselves and for our loved ones. The perils could come from fire, flood, mudslide, earthquake, windstorm, or any natural disasters that you can imagine. They might also come from events such as malicious damage, explosions, or riots. Some events are not covered in the standard policies but could be added to the insurance by paying extra premiums.

So think about all the possible risks and decide what potential risks should be insured to ensure peace of mind. The amount to insure for should allow for the rebuilding or replacement of the house and the fixtures and fittings. So, if a similar house is available on the market for $100k, or will cost $100k to rebuild, the amount to insure for the house would be $100k. If necessary, an additional amount should be included to cover expenses due to the disruption, for example, temporary rental.

Over the years we will also have accumulated a lot of belongings in the house - the household contents. These are exposed to the same risks as the house itself. They could cost a significant amount to replace and should also be insured.

Many regards buying insurance as a necessary evil. We are paying for something that we hope will never happen. So there is a good reason not to pay for insurance cover that we do not need. For example, why cover for earthquake risk for your house if your country is not anywhere near an earthquake area, or insuring for value on your house way exceeding the replacement value of the property?

The more insurance coverage is required, the higher the premium. The premium is a recurring expense that looks like a perennial, wasted expense... until there is a need to claim for compensation. So we want to insure adequately but not over-insure. The bottom line is we want to be insured for the amount we cannot afford not to be compensated for, should the risk occur.

Take for example the house insurance. If the house is 10 years old and is still in good condition, and the replacement of a similar house is available in the market for $100k, then the insured amount should not be more than $100k. To reduce the burden of the premium, the insurance policyholder could consider paying for a part of the cost before the insurance company starts to pay up. This often results in substantial premium reduction because the interest of the insuring party and the insurer are better aligned, i.e. the holder will have an incentive to minimize any risk of damages, while the insurer will have lower risks of payout. So, if there is a major fire that totally destroys the house of $100k, and if the deductible is $2k, the insurer will make a payout of $98k. But if it is a little fire that burns down a part of the wall that costs only $2k to repair, the owner will have to foot the bill.

Some choose to be self-insured for some of these common types of insurance because they have enough of their own finances to cover the particular risk.

There are many other different types of insurance coverage. Everyone should think about their own situation and the types of risks and the financial impact they potentially have, then find the insurance products that offer the desired protection. For example, someone who is involved in a business should consider buying business interruption insurance, so in the event that business income is lost due to a disaster, the insurance is able to replace that business income.

We buy insurance coverage to minimize the loss in value, or earning capacity, for our assets or the people on whom we depend. Sometimes we also have to make sure that our assets do not expose us to claims from a third party. So if a car is involved in an accident, the damage could have been inflicted by another car, but it could also have been caused by you. Car owners, therefore, do not just insure against any loss to their cars but also the loss caused to other cars. Another example is, for someone conducting business activities, public liability insurance offers financial protection against a client or member of the public who claims they have been injured, or their property damaged, because of your business activities.

Do not buy insurance from companies simply because they offer the lowest premium. Make sure the insurance companies are of great financial strength, of good reputation with a long and credible history. They should also offer both local as well as international coverage. This is to make sure they will be able to fulfil their policy obligations well into the future.

Many do not buy insurance because they think the worst will never happen or is unlikely to happen to them. It feels like an unnecessary cost because they are paying for risks that appear so remote, and for events that we hope will never happen. Taking chances has a cost, and it could well be one we can't afford.

Chapter 27
With My Best Wishes

I have lived and worked in different countries, from the developed to the less developed. I have travelled extensively, to all the continents except Antarctica. During my travels I have seen too many people who are stuck hopelessly in a financial swamp, unable to extricate themselves. I could not help feeling, if only they could do better for themselves.

For too long we lament the lack of financial literacy education. Far too many are not investing, many invest too late, too many invest with ignorance, thus finding themselves in a financially untenable situation.

I have bought stocks, and have also bought bond and mutual funds, and ETFs. I have done it myself and have also engaged the service of asset managers. I have used different brokerage platforms to trade myself, and have placed trades through intermediaries. I have gone through different boom-bust cycles. I have seen a portfolio sink by 30% or more, and portfolios remain stagnant for years. I have bought funds on the recommendations of the fund brokers that are still losing money after more than a decade. I have lived in different countries that do well and others that do not.

I learned my lessons. I hope my children do not go through the same pain. They have to take care of themselves, not be dependent on their partner or their country. The attitude of entitlement will not help achieve financial independence.

If you are a parent, you want your children to learn this. In fact, you should share this knowledge with everyone you come across. This is probably the greatest financial help you can give anyone. This is the reason I wrote this book, with my children and grandchildren in mind.

This book is put together to contain all the key aspects of a person's finances.

These are important investment tools and strategies that should belong in every person's financial toolbox. These are basic principles that are a common thread to success. I hope you have read the book, every chapter of it, and started to put together a financial plan of your own.

There are many illustrations and case studies in the book. They are done to demonstrate real actions which will bring more predictable results. I hope that through the illustrations you will more clearly see the consequence of your actions, by quantifying them in numbers. After all, what gets measured gets done. These illustrations should convince and motivate you to action. I also included the case studies to help you apply the concepts and the tools.

The book demonstrates these basic steps:

1. Set expectations – mental adjustment

2. Take care of yourself – health and habits

3. Invest in yourself – educate yourself

4. Understand basic investing principles

5. Set up financial projections

6. Craft the strategy and portfolio

7. Execute your investing strategy

8. Monitor performance and progress toward the end goals.

We pick the right ground with the right environment to sow our seeds - the fertile ground with good sunshine and abundant water. We hire the right people to tend the crops. We then give it time to grow. Likewise, we put our seed money into the right place (region/country/sector/industry/investment class) which should foster innovation, capitalism, good governance, which in turn, attracts funding from government policies. We then make sure the right people run the companies/funds. Over time, we should see results. Success is not that complicated.

No one-size fits all. We have different situations, different risk profiles. So everyone has to learn it, like other important life skills.

These good practices in the book are proven and espoused by many professionals. You can research them in more depth online. I have made many mistakes, with serious financial consequences, so hopefully, you do not have to. You may think it is daunting. It is not. It does not even have to take much time, once you start. Learning is so much easier now. So much is now online that the information you are seeking is only a click away. Just ask and it will be displayed in front of you.

The importance of financial literacy cannot be overemphasized. The scourge of poverty and financial dependencies could affect generations. So the alleviation starts with us, here and now!

Good luck.

Choon Then

(Downloadable spreadsheets can be found by writing to email **choonthen123@gmail** for an auto-reply link)

Glossary

200-day average	The average closing price of a stock over the last 200 days
401k	An employer sponsored retirement savings plan, based on a subsection of the US tax code, that allows employees to pay a portion of their salary into a long-term investment account, and where the employer may or may not choose to match some portion of that contribution.
AAPL	The stock code for Apple Inc.
Account receivables	Money owed by the customers of a business for goods or services sold.
Accounts payables	Money owed by a business to its suppliers for goods or services received.
Accumulative	A fund that reinvests the dividend instead of distributing the dividend to the investor.
Actively managed fund	A fund where the manager or management team actively manage the underlying assets of the fund, to try to optimize its performance.
Alternative Assets	A financial asset that is not one of the conventional products, namely, equity, income, cash
Alternative investment	An investment in a financial asset that is not one of the conventional products, namely, equity, income, cash.
AMD	Advanced Micro Devices, Inc., an American multinational semiconductor company
Annualized returns	The return on investment on average each year. If the investment period is less than a year or multi-years, this is scaled down to an average for 12 months.
ARK ETFs	An American investment company that manages a few ETFs, each investing in different themes in the disruptive technology sectors. The fund mangers actively look for prospective targets instead of passively tracking the indexes.

ARKF	One of the Ark family of ETFs that invests in disruptive Fintech sector.
ARKG	One of the Ark family of ETFs that invests in the genomic revolution.
ARKK	One of the Ark family of ETFs that invests in disruptive Fintech sector.
ARKW	One of the Ark family of ETFs that invests in next generation internet.
Asset Management companies	Firms that invest pooled funds from retail and institutional investors and invest them in various tradeable financial assets, e.g. stocks, bonds.
Asset Managers	A finance professional who helps others to manage their assets.
Asset under management	The total market value of the investments that a person or company manages for the clients.
AUM	Acronym for Asset Under Management. The total market value of the investments that a person or company manages for the clients.
Balance Sheet	The financial statement of a company that states the ending balances of the assets, liabilities and shareholder equity at a certain point in time.
Betterment	An American financial advisory company which provides robo-advisory service.
Big Tech	Major large technology companies with dominant positions in the US, including Google, Amazon, Apple, Meta (Facebook), and Microsoft.
Biotech	Technology based on biology, that uses living organisms or systems to solve problems and produce products that improve the quality of human life.
Blackrock	An American multinational investment management. The world's largest asset manager.
Bloomberg	A US media company that provides financial news and information, research, and financial data to the world.

Blue chip stock	Stocks of typically large, well-known, high-quality companies, financially sound companies that have operated for many years and are leaders in their industries.
Board of Directors	A panel of people elected to represent and protect shareholders interest. It is the highest governing authority within the management structure, typically meets at regular intervals to set corporate management and oversight policies.
Bonds	A fixed-income instrument, issued by the borrowers, such as a company, to the lenders, as a financial instrument of indebtedness to the holders.
Brexit	A portmanteau of the words Britain and exit, when Britain left the European Union on 1st January 2020.
Brokerage platform	Software used for trading securities like stocks and ETFs, through a financial intermediary such as an online broker.
Capital (in Balance Sheet)	Cash paid into the company by investors to buy the company's stock.
Capital gains	When the price of selling the asset is more than the price of the purchase.
Cash from financing activities (in Cashflow Statement)	A section of the Cashflow Statement that shows the inflows and outflows of cash from the business financing activities, i.e. cash in and out flows that affect the equity capital and borrowing structure of a company, for example, adding loans, selling more stock, paying dividend.
Cash from investing activities (in Cashflow Statement)	A section of the Cashflow Statement that shows cash generated or spent relating to investment activities. These include acquisition and disposition of long-term assets such as companies, properties, plants and equipment.
Cash from operating activities (in Cashflow Statement)	A section of the Cashflow Statement that shows the cashflow earned from operating activities, i.e. its regular business activities.

Cashflow Statement	A financial report in summarized form that provides details on what happened to the cash situation of the business during a specific period of time, including during what cash flows into and out of the company, from its business operation, financing and investing activities.
Central banks	A financial institution of the state, responsible for overseeing the monetary system and policy of a nation, including the money supply and availability of credit; overseeing the commercial banking system; and acting as emergency lenders to distressed banks. In the U.S. is known as the Federal Reserve.
CEO	Chief Executive Officer, the highest ranking executive of the company, that has the chief managerial decision-making authority.
CFO	The Chief Financial Officer, the top financial position in an organization, responsible for overseeing the financial activities of an entire company.
Charles Schwab	An American multinational financial services company that offers banking, an electronic trading platform, and wealth management advisory services.
CNBC	An American pay television business news channel offering live and global financial market information and programming.
CNBC- Fast Money and Half Time	Business and investment programs by CNBC.
Commodity	A basic good, usually a resource, used as an input in the production of goods and services. It often has the characteristic of being interchangeable with other goods of the same type.
Compound annual growth rate	A measure of an investment's annual growth rate over time, with compounding effect.
Compounding Effects	The effect of earnings generated by an asset is itself generating earnings, creating a snowballing effect.
Consumption tax	Tax on the consumption of goods and services.
Corporate tax	Tax on the profits of a corporation.

Cost of goods sold	Cost of goods that are either manufactured or purchased and then sold.
CPF	Singapore's mandatory social security savings scheme funded by contributions from employers and employees.
CQQQ	An ETF that invests mainly in the China technology sector.
Credit score	Credit score is a measure used in many countries to determine the creditworthiness of an individual.
Currency exchange rates	The rate at which one currency is exchanged for another currency.
Current price (of stock/ETF)	The most recent the stock/ETF is trading for in the market.
Custody fee	Fee charged by the banks or brokerages to mange our investment accounts, including facilitating our payments for securities purchased, the purchased securities placed in our account, receiving dividends, and keeping the assets safe.
Derivative products	Financial contracts between two or more parties whose value is based on an agreed-upon underlying financial asset which could include bonds, commodities, currencies, interest rates, market indexes, and stocks.
Dimension ETFs.	ETFs, including actively managed ETFs, offered by the Dimensional Fund Advisors, a well known US investment firm.
Discretionary spending	Money spent on nonessential things. Non-essential things are things a household or company can survive without.
Distributing	Distributing are funds that distribute dividends to its investors (as opposed to, for example, Accumulating, which is funds that reinvest the investor's dividends within the fund).
Diversification	A strategy to mitigate risk so that the financial impact on the total asset is reduced as a result of not concentrating the risks on just one stock, one sector, one industry, one asset class, one country.

Dividend tax	Tax imposed on the dividend received by the investor.
Dividend yield	Dividend paid out by a company expressed as a percentage of its share price.
DIY	Do-it-yourself.
Dollar-cost averaging	The strategy of spreading out stock or fund purchases, buying at regular intervals and in roughly equal amounts.
Domicile (fund)	Where the fund's holding company is incorporated, and therefore usually also where the management of the fund is located.
Dow (market index)	Short for Dow Jones Industrial Average, it is a benchmark that tracks 30 of the largest American blue-chip stocks listed in the Nasdaq and New York Stock Exchange. These are subjectively picked.
Earnings growth	The increase, or decrease, in a company's earnings between two periods.
Earnings	Net profit or net income. This is calculated by subtracting from the revenue all the business expenditures, including the cost of the goods sold, the selling and administration expenses, interest, taxes.
Emerging markets	Economies that are experiencing rapid growth but have not reached their full potential to be developed economies.
Employee stocks purchase plan	A company-run plan for employees to buy shares in the company at a discount to market price, thereby participate in the success of the company.
EPF	Employee Provident Fund - a Malaysian Government enforced compulsory retirement savings fund for employees in the private sector.
EPS	Earnings per share, calculated as a company's profit divided by the number of outstanding shares.
Equity (investment)	Money invested in a company's shares.
ESG	Acronym for environmental, social, and governance, a set of used by socially conscious investors to screen investments which have a policy of sustainability.

Estate tax	Tax on assets that pass from the deceased to the beneficiaries.
ETF	Exchange Traded Fund, a fund that contains a basket of securities that tracks an index, sector, commodity, or other asset, but which can be purchased or sold on a stock exchange much like stock.
Expense ratio	A measure of how much expense is incurred by the fund manager in managing the fund, relative to the size of the asset under management. It is calculated by dividing the total expenses incurred by the average value of the portfolio.
FAANG	An acronym for Facebook (now Meta), Amazon, Apple, Netflix, and Google (now Alphabet), among the largest and well known of the big technology companies.
Federal Reserve	The central bank of the US. Its functions include maximizing employment, stabilizing prices, moderating long-term interest rates, supervising banks, maintaining the stability of the financial system, and providing financial services to depository institutions, the U.S. government, and foreign official institutions.
Fidelity	An American multinational financial services company, one of the world's largest asset managers, offering a diversified investment brokerage, offering the full range of investment products.
Financial Planner	A financial advisor who helps their clients build a plan and to meet their long term financial goals.
Financial planner fee	Fee charged by a Financial Planner who helps their clients build a plan and to meet their long term financial goals.
Financial statements	A set of financial reports that summarizes the financial positions and activities of a business, company or entity.
Fintech	Financial Technology that uses modern technology to improve financial services.
Fixed assets (in Balance Sheet)	Assets used in the company's operation to generate income that has a useful life of more than a year.
Fund (management) fee	Fee charged by the fund manager for managing the investment fund.

Fund company	Companies that own, manage and sell funds to the public.
Fund performance	The return achieved by the fund.
Fund size	The amount of the asset the fund is managing.
Fund strategy	The approach used by the fund manager to invest clients' money.
Fundamentals (of stocks/investment)	Factors that affect the intrinsic value of an investment.
Gross Domestic Products (GDP)	The value of goods and services produced in a country in a specific period
Gross margin	Profit made after subtracting the cost of goods that are either manufactured or purchased and then sold , from the revenue.
Growth stock	A stock that is expected to grow its revenue or profit significantly faster than the average by other companies in the industry or the market.
Guidance (issued by companies)	A company's public estimates of its current-quarter and future earnings outlook, usually immediately after the past quarter's earning release.
Health savings plan	A personal saving and investment plan set up to pay for a person's health care expenses.
Hedge fund	A pooled investment fund catering to the high-net-worth-individuals and institutional investors, often relying on complex techniques to build its portfolio and manage risk, such as short selling, leverage, and derivatives.
Hedging	A strategy to reduce the risks to an investment.
High Net Worth Individual	Designated by some in the finance industry of individuals with assets of a substantial amount that can easily be converted into cash, typically at least USD 1m.
Inception (funds/ETFs)	When the funds become available to the public.
Independent directors	Members of the board of directors who are not part of the company's executive team and are not involved with the day-to-day operations of the company. They help the company with their diverse skill and experience, and improve corporate credibility and governance.

Index (market)	A measure of stock market performance, computed from the prices of a basket of selected securities such as stocks.
Inflation	Increase in prices of goods and services.
Inflation rate	The percentage change in the increase in cost of goods and services, compared with a previous period.
Insurance policy	A contract between the insurer and the purchaser of the insurance coverage.
Insurance premium	The amount paid to insurers to obtain insurance coverage.
Interactive Brokers	An American multinational brokerage firm that also operates one of the largest trading platforms.
Internal auditors	Consultants independent of the company's operations who evaluate the company's operations and report to the highest level in the organization. Typically they report to the board of directors, the accounting officer or the audit committee.
Inventory	Raw materials, finished and unfinished products still held in the company.
IPO	Initial Public Offering (IPO) - when a private corporation sells it stock to the public for the first time.
IVV	An ETF that track the performance of the S&P 500.
IWDA	The iShares Core MSCI World ETF, traded in the London Stock Exchange, investing in companies across the globe.
Liabilities (in Balance Sheet)	Money that a company owes to outside parties, including amounts owed to suppliers of goods and services, employees and lenders.
Market cap	Market capitalization, i.e. the total dollar market value of a company, by multiplying its stock's current market price by the total number of shares that can be bought and sold by the public.
Mega-Tech	A few of the largest of the big US technology companies which are well known and dominant in their sectors.

Mutual funds

Investment funds consisting of securities (stocks, bonds, etc) managed by fund managers, using funds pooled from investors. They usually actively buy and sell securities as they see fit.

Nasdaq

The Nasdaq Composite is a stock market index that includes almost all stocks listed on the Nasdaq stock exchange. Heavily weighted towards companies in the information technology sector.

Net Operating profit

Earnings made after subtracting the cost of goods sold from the revenue, as well as the selling and administration expenses, and tax.

Net Profit after tax

Earnings after subtracting all expenses and tax.

Net Profit before tax

Earnings after subtracting all expenses but before tax.

Opec

The Organization of the Petroleum Exporting Countries (OPEC), made up of 13 of the world's major oil exporting countries to coordinate policies for its members.

Other income/Expenses

Income that does not come from a company's main business or losses not related to the normal course of the company.

Outperform

When a stock or ETF is projected to provide returns higher than the market average.

Passive investing

Investing by automatically selecting the underlying investment securities to match the index it chooses to track. It does not involve any active stock/ETF picking to try to outperform the index.

Passively managed fund

A fund where the investment securities are not chosen by the fund manager but instead are automatically selected to match an index or section of the market.

PE

Price-to-earnings ratio - measures the company's share price relative to its earnings per share.

PE (forward)

Price-to-earnings ratio - measures the company's share price relative to its future estimated earnings per share.

Personal income tax

Income tax individuals pay on their salary and other income.

Pharma	Pharmaceutical companies collectively as a sector or industry.
Portfolio	A collection of financial investments, including stocks, bonds, commodities, cash, real estate, art, etc.
Portfolio allocation	The process of allocating money to realize the portfolio makeup desired.
Price Earning ratio	A measure of a stock's valuation (PE), using the formula share price/earnings per share for the year. EPS is the earnings/number of shares of a company.
Private banking	Personalized financial services, including investment, banking and other, offered to the wealthier clients.
Profit and Loss Statement	A financial statement that summarizes how a business generates profit from its revenue, plus the costs and the expenses it incurred during the period.
Public companies	A company whose shares are traded freely on a stock exchange.
Rating agencies	Firms that assesses the financial strength and rating services of their target companies and government, for a fee. Investors use the ratings as a guide on whether or not to buy the securities offered for purchase.
Retained Earnings	Retained earnings are an accumulation of a company's net income and net losses over all the years the business has been in operation.
Return on investment (ROI)	A simple ratio to evaluate how an investment has performed, calculated by dividing the profit by the investment cost.
Revenue growth	The increase, or decrease, in a company's sales between two periods.
Robinhood	A US online brokerage popular for its commission-free trading on its mobile trading patform.
Robo-advisors	Digital platforms that provide automated investment services driven by algorithms based on some modern portfolio theory with little to no human supervision.

Russell (market index)	An index that includes a wide number of US companies. The index could include 1000 to 3000 of these companies, and therefore could include not only the leading and largest companies, but also the mid-range and smaller-sized companies.
S&P 500	A stock market index tracking the performance of 500 leading companies listed on the US stock exchanges, widely used to indicate the performance of the broader US stock market.
Sales commission (of mutual fund)	Commission paid by investors of mutual funds to financial intermediaries such as agents, financial planners, advisors for selling the fund.
Sales Revenue	Revenue from sales of products and services.
SEC	The U.S. Securities and Exchange Commission, an independent agency of the US government responsible for making sure the security market functions properly and protects investors.
Sector	A grouping of companies or stocks in similar industries doing business that provide similar goods and services.
Securities	Tradable financial assets or instrument that have value and can be bought, sold, or traded between parties. These include stocks, bonds, mutual funds and ETFs.
Securities and Exchange	The U.S. Securities and Exchange Commission, an independent agency of the US government responsible for making sure the security market functions properly and protects investors.
Selling and Admin expenses	All everyday operating expenses of running a business. Includes nearly all business costs not covered in the category of 'cost of goods sold'.
Small-cap	Companies with small market capitalization, i.e. the value of the shares in public hands is relatively smaller than the mid-cap and large-cap. Some professionals consider the value to be between $300m to $2 billion.
Sub-sector	One of different sectors within a sector. A sector is a grouping of companies or stocks in similar industries doing business that provide similar goods and services.

Subsidized retirement scheme	A retirement plan subsidized by the government or company, with their matching part of the individual's contribution or the granting of tax benefits, to encourage saving for retirement.
Target price	Analysts' projection of a stock's future price.
Ticker symbol	It is generally English letters unique to the specific assets or securities listed on a stock exchange and are used to identify a specific product for trading purposes.
Trading fee	Fee paid to the broker to help facilitate trading done, e.g. buying and selling of stocks, through the platform.
UBS	A Swiss multinational investment bank and financial services company.
Valuation (of stock/company)	The method to try to determine the intrinsic value of the stock/company.
Vanguard	The second-largest issuer of exchange-traded funds in the world.
VGT	Vanguard Information Technology Index Fund ETF. An ETF that focuses on tracking the performance of the information technology sector.
VHT	Vanguard Health Care Index Fund ETF. An ETF that tracks the healthcare index.
VOO	Vanguard 500 Index Fund ETF. An ETF tracking the S&P 500.
VUSD	Vanguard S&P 500 UCITS ETF USD. An ETF that tracks the S&P 500 that is domiciled in Ireland.
Wealth Manager	Investment advisory service that provides bundled financial services such as investment advice, tax services, legal or estate planning, and retirement planning, to affluent clients.
Wealthfront	One of the most well-known US robo-advisors.